Redefining
Staff Development

A Collaborative

Model

for Teachers

and Administrators

Laura Robb

HEINEMANN

Portsmouth, NH

Heinemann
A division of Reed Elsevier Inc.
361 Hanover Street
Portsmouth, NH 03801–3912
www.heinemann.com

Offices and agents throughout the world

The author and publisher wish to thank those who have generously given permission to reprint borrowed material:

"The Prayer of the Ox" from *Prayers from the Ark* by Carmen Bernos de Gasztold, translated by Rumer Godden, copyright © 1962, renewed 1990 by Rumer Godden. Original Copyright 1947, © 1955 by Editions du Cloitre. Used by permission of Viking Penguin, a division of Penguin Putnam Inc., and Curtis Brown.

"The Pasture" by Robert Frost from *The Poetry of Robert Frost,* edited by Edward Connery Lathem. Copyright 1939, © 1967, 1969 by Henry Holt & Company. Reprinted by permission of Henry Holt and Company, LLC.

"The Pasture" by Robert Frost from *The Poetry of Robert Frost,* edited by Edward Connery Lathem, published by Jonathan Cape. Reprinted by permission of Random House Archive & Library.

Library of Congress Cataloging-in-Publication Data
Robb, Laura
    Redefining staff development : a collaborative model for teachers and administrators /
Laura Robb.
        p. cm.
    Includes bibliographical references.
    ISBN 0-325-00214-2 (paperback)
    1. Teachers—Inservice training. 2. School personnel management. I. Title.
LB1731 .R55   2000
370'.71'55—dc21

00-039537

Editor: Danny Miller
Production: Vicki Kasabian
Cover design: Michael Leary
Manufacturing: Deanna Richardson

Printed in the United States of America on acid-free paper
04   03   DA   5

For my son, Evan, with deepest love, respect, and pride
And for Ann Conners, John Lathrop, and Nancy Lee

Contents

Acknowledgments

My philosophy of professional study has been greatly influenced by collaborations with principals and teachers at schools where I teach, coach, and lead study groups.

First, I am grateful to John Lathrop, Head of Powhatan School in Boyce, Virginia, and all of my terrific, supportive colleagues who collaborated with me to create innovative, yet sound and meaningful professional study programs. Their candid feedback and honesty in expressing needs and adjustments enabled us to build community, construct a meaningful peer-evaluation program, try many variations of study groups, grow professionally, and support children's learning.

Deepest thanks go to principal Ann Conners, assistant principal Joe Nicholas, and all the dedicated teachers at Keister Elementary School in Harrisonburg, Virginia. Through conversations, study groups, e-mail correspondence, and team teaching, we created professional study programs and teacher partnerships that enabled all of us to grow professionally and helped the children we serve improve.

Sincere thanks to Nikki Isherwood, Director of Instruction for Winchester City Schools in Winchester, Virginia. Nikki understood the goals and benefits of teacher study groups and invited me to collaborate with teachers. One incredible learning experience for me was the study group that included teachers from Winchester's primary grades and middle school. Nikki believed that a deeper understanding of literacy development would occur with a range of grade levels. How right she was! I also learned so much from training and working alongside Winchester's lead teachers.

Thanks to Nancy Lee, principal of Quarles Elementary School in Winchester, for encouraging me to develop an early literacy intervention program and literacy study groups at her school.

I am grateful to Jane Gaidos, principal of W. W. Robinson Elementary School in Woodstock, Virginia. Her honesty with teachers and me has been the basis of a professional study collaboration that enabled me to grow and support her teachers.

To my son, Evan, deepest thanks for dialoguing with me and sharing parts of his journal as he prepared to open, as principal, Warren County Junior High School, a new building in Front Royal, Virginia. His thoughtful questions and constant probing nudged me to revise and clarify ideas and search for creative and inexpensive ways to help teachers grow as professionals. How proud I am that being a principal who supports teachers, children, and parents has become his lifelong passion.

Sincere thanks to William Flora, assistant superintendent of Warren County Public Schools, for reading and commenting on parts of the book and for sharing his philosophy about professional study and learning.

Anina, my daughter, who teaches middle school in New York City, how I appreciate and thank you for those long telephone conversations when you shared staff development experiences and reacted to ideas I raised.

To Ray Coutu, who persisted in encouraging me to pursue this topic, my thanks for believing in me and the need for this book. Ray nudged me to complete the lengthy proposal and helped the seed grow into a book.

And thanks to Danny Miller, my editor at Heinemann; I am grateful for his honest feedback and constant attention to the manuscript. A joy to work with, Danny has offered the support and insight a writer needs and longs for. Always respectful of my voice, ideas, and beliefs about professional study, Danny quickly responded to my queries and offered excellent suggestions that improved the book.

The greatest thanks go to my husband, Lloyd, who never complained about the hours I devoted to writing. Lloyd read all of the drafts, offering me valuable input, and spent hours conversing about issues with me. Our dialoguing clarified many ideas and made the writing even more enjoyable.

Introduction

"Have you taught and responded to children for twenty years or have you repeated your first two years for the past twenty?"

I posed this question to myself after my first year of teaching in a small public school in rural Virginia. That year, I bumped into a teaching strategy that still exists: develop a set of lessons, tests, and quizzes during your first year or two, and your teaching career is set. Simply repeat the plans again and again. Boring for teachers and boring for students, such a strategy creates a stale and static school culture—a culture isolated from the growth and change in educational research, the community surrounding the school, the society, and the world.

The moment the question invaded my mind, I jotted the words onto paper. Today, that question is posted on a bulletin board next to my computer. It's a reminder that to be an effective teacher, I must continue to learn, problem solve, and respond to the evolving needs of my students.

I frequently ask this question, adding five, ten, and fifteen years to it, when I start working with a school. Inviting teachers and administrators to reflect on it can reveal much about the way children learn, how the adults view learning, and the level of collaboration among administrators, teachers, parents, and students.

I open with a question because I believe that when teachers inquire, when they pose questions about their needs, frustrations, and hopes and continue questioning as they learn and apply new practices in their classroom, a culture of inquiry, reflection, and self-evaluation develops. Inquiry identifies problems and issues within a school and allows teachers and administrators to develop professional study experiences that address these problems, taking teachers where they are and gently journeying them to other places.

Posing questions about teaching and learning has continued throughout my professional life, which started the summer of 1963 when I left New York City to live in Winchester, Virginia. In New York, I worked as a copywriter, but in Winchester, a small southern town, there were no jobs for me.

1

Encouraged by my husband, I accepted a job teaching sixth grade in a rural elementary school. I replaced the principal's wife, who had had surgery a week before school opened and was on medical leave for one year. With no education courses and a degree in English and French literature, I learned from and with thirty sixth graders because my observations and questions drove my teaching; they still do today.

That year teaching claimed me, and my enthusiasm for learning and teaching has not waned. For more than thirty-five years, I have taught in grades four to eight at Powhatan, an independent elementary school in rural Boyce, Virginia. Twelve years ago, I started coaching teachers in kindergarten through eighth grade. Without those years of experience, I could not nurture and support teachers nor stand in their shoes.

Today, I spend three days a week at Powhatan School teaching an eighth-grade reading-writing workshop, coaching teachers, and organizing professional study. In addition, I write professional articles and books, consult with three public school systems in Virginia, and sometimes teach a graduate class for an area university or school district. Life is full and busy, but I always make sure there's time to do things I love: spend time with family, hike, listen to music, attend concerts, and read. The fuller and more balanced my life is, the more I have to bring to my professional work as teachers and I learn together all year in professional study programs.

You might wonder why I use the phrase *professional study* instead of *staff development.* Teachers who engage in professional study expand their knowledge of teaching practices and how children learn by integrating reading, reflecting, and collaborating into school life. Staff development, the foil to professional study, is often presented as one experience in time, when an authority on a topic crams information into teachers' minds with little to no knowledge of the school's culture and varied needs. Such presentations deter inquiry because one-time staff development programs do not respond to teachers' questions, nor do they provide the follow-up necessary to create growth and change.

Inquiry-based professional study within a school creates a teacher-centered learning environment that recognizes and respects the differences in teachers' theoretical backgrounds, prior knowledge, familiarity with children's literature, classroom experiences, and expertise. Professional study events in a teacher-centered environment include question posing, conversations, hands-on experiences, journal writing, and what Gordon Wells calls *storying,* creating stories in the mind to link past experiences to new ones. With these five fundamental ways of constructing meaning, learning among teachers becomes a collaborative and shared experience.

In addition to inquiry, choice is necessary for professional study to be an effective mode of growth and change. Choice is at the heart of making a commitment: an invitation to join a study group or work with a peer respects teachers' right to accept or decline. It also allows teachers who are skeptical about change to be observers and listeners and to talk to colleagues who are actively involved in professional learning before making a personal commitment.

You can legislate that teachers join a study group, but you can't ensure that they'll read professional literature, participate in group discussions, or try new strategies. One fifth grader summed up legislated learning this way: "My mom and dad make me read every night. I know how to keep my eyes on the page and when to turn pages so they think I'm reading. You know what I'm doing? I'm thinking of kicking a soccer ball or which TV program I'll watch for a reward."

A principal who integrates ongoing professional study into daily life can renew and energize teachers, inspiring them to change classroom environments and teaching practices for the purpose of improving the ways children learn. Such change is even more likely to occur when professional study encourages teachers to continually pose questions, reflect, self-evaluate, and collaborate to problem solve. In such a school culture, teachers think about their teaching, learning, and the kinds of experiences they offer children.

To accomplish significant change in a school community, administrators must help teachers carve out time for sharing and reflection without creating stress and frustration. The purpose of this book is to present effective, ongoing professional study programs from several elementary and middle schools. Detailing how and why these programs started, the revision process teachers and administrators used to improve them, and how teachers' learning ultimately affects students' learning, this book will present a menu of ideas that can help you plan and initiate professional study suited to your school's culture.

Several times a year, I read "The Prayer of the Ox" from *Prayers from the Ark* (1973), by Carmen Bernos de Gasztold, to administrators, teachers, students, and myself. These prayers, spoken by Noah's animals, are not pleas but expressions of each animal's problems. For the ox as well as teachers, lack of time is a great problem. The poem cautions educators that traveling the path of professional study as a lifelong learner takes time, and the ox shows us the dual benefit of plodding and slowing down: time to think and opportunity to digest ideas.

> Dear God, give me time
> Men are always so driven!

Make them understand that I can never hurry.
Give me time to eat.
Give me time to plod.
Give me time to sleep.
Give me time to think.

Amen

1

From Traditional Staff Development to Professional Study

Many years ago, I attended a half-day inservice on reading, which was required for middle-grade teachers. Before the program began, teachers gathered for coffee. Everyone was looking forward to the session because teachers had requested a speaker who would present practical reading strategies that could be applied across the curriculum. Prior to his visit, the speaker had not talked to nor surveyed teachers. The principal introduced the speaker and left after the first fifteen minutes. Soon I noticed some teachers doodling. Others closed their eyes. Many repeatedly looked at their watches.

The speaker primed me and my colleagues with state and national statistics on elementary school reading scores, then presented an overview of tests that measured reading skills. During the presentation, he flashed more than fifty overheads filled with print so small no one could read it.

After the midmorning break, empty chairs dotted the room. Many teachers had departed, mumbling, "What does all this have to do with my students?" and "Another wasted morning," and "I could use this time to work in my room."

The morning dragged on, no different from most inservice lectures I had attended over the years. But I was different. My teaching life had informed me that the delivery model of casting wisdom to passive participants didn't work with children. Why should it work with teachers or anyone else who wanted to learn?

Instead of turning to my usual tuning-out strategies of mulling over the mystery I was reading or jotting down a list of chores to complete in the evening, that inservice nudged me into a questioning mode. This is what I wrote on my yellow legal pad:

1. Why is this so dreadfully boring?
2. Do adults learn differently from children?
3. How can we change these one-size-fits-all presentations?
4. What do I want to learn about reading?
5. What do I need to help my students improve as readers?
6. What does improving as a reader have to do with lifetime reading?
7. Don't we teachers deserve choices? How would choice change staff development?
8. Have any of us asked students what they think they need to improve?
9. Has an administrator asked teachers what we need to grow and change?
10. Is what I want to learn the same as what my colleagues want and need?

As soon as I posed the tenth question, I recognized that staff development is a complex concept and that shifts in theory and practice could never occur in a one-shot, one-size-fits-all presentation. As I reread the questions on my yellow legal pad, comments spoken by colleagues after attending inservice sessions bombarded my mind:

"I want follow-up support—someone to watch me teach and answer my questions."

"When will we learn by *doing?* If I'm going to try something new, I need to see and *feel* how it works."

"Are there articles or books out there that can help me?"

"What a wasted day! I've learned nothing I can bring back to my students."

"This person hasn't been inside a classroom for fifteen years. How can he help me?"

"I want to see students' work, not a list of statistics."

"Some of the information seemed worthwhile. But there was too much. By lunchtime, I couldn't focus on another idea."

These remarks highlight teachers' frustrations and point to a need to question, rethink, and revise the traditional staff development model.

The Traditional Staff Development Model

Before plunging into transforming traditional staff development, it's crucial to clearly understand the components of the model and how each one inhibits professional growth.

One-day teacher training   Even if a school holds two to three inservice sessions a year, they are usually ineffective because sessions do not account for the differing levels of expertise and knowledge among staff members. Moreover, at these sessions, presenters tend to overload teachers with information. Teachers depart confused, not knowing which strategy to try; they file away mounds of handouts and eventually add them to a recycling bin.

One-size-fits-all presentation   Administrators spend huge amounts of staff development budget and hire an outside "expert" who knows little to nothing about a school's teachers, students, and culture. Hawking a prepackaged program, the expert steps into a school, lectures for several hours, then travels to other schools, repeating the presentation.

Minimal administrator participation   Principals who briefly pop into inservice sessions or don't attend because of pressing paperwork or meetings send the message that this session is unimportant. These administrators deprive themselves of opportunities to study, discuss, think, and continually confront and revise their theory of learning. When principals' actions demonstrate that lifelong learning and keeping abreast of research are important, they inspire their teachers to study and take risks.

Lack of follow-up support   Most often there is not enough money to invite the "expert" back to assist teachers who risk trying new ideas. Moreover, principals who cling to the traditional inservice model have not confronted the issue of how and why people learn. Absent from sessions, they lack the direct experience that could enable them to understand the need for strong follow-up systems.

In spite of these drawbacks, year after year, school administrators spend precious budget money for inservice teacher training without questioning whether real and meaningful growth can occur.

Changing the Traditional Staff Development Model

Some administrators have begun to confront the ineffectiveness of the traditions they inherited. Ann Conners, principal of Keister Elementary School in Harrisonburg, Virginia, wanted ongoing support for her teachers. When she invited me to coach, team teach, and organize monthly study groups, Ann said, "I want my teachers involved in deciding what they need to learn. I want them to develop into teachers who respond to children who change as the year unfolds. I don't want recipes. I want a long-term program so you and teachers have the time to collaborate and learn together."

"Let's complete and assess one year," I replied. "If teachers feel comfortable learning with me and want me to return, then I'll extend my commitment. At the end of one year, I want teachers to anonymously complete a survey that asks them to evaluate the effectiveness of study groups, class collaborations, and one-on-one follow-up conversations, as well as suggest needs and ways to improve professional study. We can use their responses to explore ways to improve the collaboration and make a decision about my return."

"How can we make this work?" Ann asked.

"During the first year, I want to invite teachers to work with me in their classrooms," I told Ann. We brainstormed possible schedules and decided that during my visits I'd be in three classrooms in the morning and provide individual feedback during the afternoon.

Whenever our monthly study-group sessions replaced a scheduled faculty meeting, Ann required that teachers attend. This would be another opportunity for the staff to interact with me as we practiced and discussed reading and writing strategies. Our hope was that after several study-group sessions, I'd receive many invitations from teachers.

"What if no one accepts your invitation?" Ann immediately asked. "Only the three of us who took your summer class know something about you."

"First, during a scheduled meeting, I'll work with the entire faculty, explain my role in the school, and invite them to question me. Then I'll divide teachers into grade-level teams to raise questions about instruction, curriculum, teaching needs, and the kinds of support they'd like. Based on past experiences, I'm sure when you extend the invitation, some of the teachers will accept."

However, I clearly understood that my salary was for a full day's work, so I suggested that I administer individual reading assessments and running records if I had time. Supporting teachers was another way to open communication and build trust, I told Ann.

Administrative Guidelines for Effective Professional Study

At the close of my meeting with Ann Conners, I emphasized four points:

1. Since administrators will be responsible for follow-up support, Ann Conners, Joe Nicholas (the assistant principal), and resource teachers must actively participate in the study-group sessions I lead and those that teachers organize.

2. So all teachers can attend study groups, sessions should replace a required faculty meeting. If a study group for specific grades is facilitated by a consultant, those teachers attending should be excused from that week's faculty meeting. Colleagues can fill teachers in on missed information or teachers can read the minutes from a faculty meeting.

3. If administrators ask teachers to give up their own time in the morning or after school to attend study groups, teachers should have the choice of accepting, declining, or attending only some of the meetings.

4. To create a professional environment where teachers feel their efforts have been recognized, the principal should work with the superintendent to offer recertification credits and/or continuing-education units for professional study. Some school districts work with an area university and arrange graduate credit for yearlong study.

This conversation with Ann Conners is one I repeat with all school administrators before I commit to a trial year in a school. I want administrators to be aware that professional study takes time—there are no instant remedies. When administrators collaborate with teachers and create ongoing programs, they empower themselves and members of a school community to become self-directed learners.

Moreover, it's the *doing* that leads administrators to the conclusion that change needs time. If principals are to move beyond their past experiences and present assumptions about how teachers learn, they must read and study to construct new knowledge that can change their thinking about learning. Principals can join teacher study groups and form their own study groups in which they share the successes and problems of professional study programs in their schools (Evans and Mohr 1999).

The Benefits of Conversations

Ann and I created a first-year schedule of six visits that allowed me to team teach or observe three teachers in the mornings. During the afternoons, one substitute teacher covered each teacher's class successively, so I could attend three thirty-minute conferences.

The afternoon conferring time enabled me to spotlight what worked in the morning, raise questions to engage the teacher in a meaningful discussion, and share strategies. Ann Conners, Joe Nicholas, and the teacher's team leader were available for follow-up feedback and support between my six visits.

A Classroom Visit and Follow-Up Conversation

One week before I drove to Keister, teachers faxed me letters that described what they were doing in their classrooms. They also raised questions that enabled me to prepare for my visit. The following are excerpts from letters written by fourth-grade teacher Ann Lintner as well as portions of our follow-up conversations.

Questions Anne Lintner Posed

1. I often feel I am shortchanging writing, reading, or word study. I continue to try to integrate the three, but am not yet satisfied with the schedule. What schedule has worked well for you?

2. How can I find more time to conference individually with students on reading? How can I improve the quality of book club discussions while I'm working with one group and others are discussing on their own?

3. How can I get students to be more responsible for solving spelling problems in their writing?

My Preparation for Follow-Up Meeting

Based on Anne's questions, I brought the following:

1. Sample schedules of other teachers' reading-writing workshops.

2. "Have-a-Go" sheets. This is a strategy adapted from Australia (Parry and Hornsby 1988) that assumes children, like adults, can pinpoint a misspelled word even if they cannot spell it. From their daily writing, children select misspelled words and "have a go," two to three times, at conventional spellings. In a short conference, the teacher follows up with a student to scaffold thinking processes and to lead the child to conventional spelling. Adults use this strategy when they write a word several times, using their visual memory to figure out standard spelling.

3. Focus Conference Records for Reading/Writing. I developed this record form (see Appendix A) for *Easy-to-Manage Reading & Writing Conferences* (1998).

The following is an excerpt from a conversation between Anne Lintner and me.

Laura: How did you feel about today's lesson?

Anne: I worked with all four word-study groups, but it was exhausting.

Laura: You did work with all groups and you did a great job. I noticed that you had detailed plans for groups who were reading or doing word study on their own.

Anne: I want them to be doing worthwhile things and also stay busy so I can get to every group. I spend hours at home planning this.

Laura: Here are some workshop schedules for you to study and compare to your own. You might consider trying word study three times a week, meeting with two groups each period, and creating a rotation plan. You'll see all four groups every two days.

Anne: But what about the rest of the class?

Laura: I think what you want the students to do is great—read, write, and work on word study. But you're doing all the planning and thinking. I'd like to see your students involved in that.

Anne: But how?

Laura: For independent word study, you can have students work on four to five misspelled words from their writing, then complete the "Have-a-Go" sheet. [I explain how the strategy works.]

Anne: How can I get book discussions to be more meaningful? I give groups questions and journal responses, but I have to make up several sets of plans because they read different books.

Laura: It's great that you have students reading different books at their independent levels. Students told me they loved the books and all of them seemed engrossed in their reading. You might want to try the "center stage" technique (Robb 1998) we practiced last week during our study-group session, when four teachers sat in front of the group and discussed a story. I coached them by asking *What made you say that? Can you support that idea with the text? Does anyone have a different idea? Does anyone disagree?* It's a great opportunity for you to help students see what a meaningful book discussion looks like and to learn how to keep the conversation going. While a group takes center stage and converses in front of the class, I always ask observers to take notes on what worked. I note my observations on an overhead transparency and share with the class. It's a great way to build on what students do well.

A week later, Anne sent me this e-mail:

Dear Laura,

I so appreciated your prompt reply in sending the upper level word study information I spoke of. I had a chance to look at it this morning and will be able to better meet the needs of my upper level spellers this spring using the lists . . . I did only model one sort this week . . . hurrah . . . and the kids are on their own. I chose the middle group of words. I also used the "Have-a-Go" sheet last week, and we pulled some words from our writing. We will use some of those this week.

I'm going to try short, focused ten minute reading conferences with individual students. I put one literature discussion group on "center stage" on Monday and we all observed their discussion regarding the fantasy books we finished. I recorded my observations on the overhead and they wrote notes on paper. You were right, other groups volunteered to go next. I will decrease my planning for individual groups and will do more modeling and circulating. Thanks for your encouragement and your support.

Anne Lintner

Reflection led Anne to sift through her teaching practices and frame questions that illuminated the places she wanted to go as a teacher. Anne used talk and writing to deepen and clarify her understanding of how to revise and adjust her teaching.

Communicating Between Visits

During the weeks between my monthly visits, teachers conversed with me through e-mail, and together we tried to solve problems that arose. The back-and-forth writing often built a trusting relationship and held the potential for nudging teachers forward. The following is a sampling of "Dear Laura" e-mail correspondence.

Teacher: I've started one-on-one reading conferences during SSR [sustained silent reading]. Can't keep them to 10 minutes. We get talking and the bell rings and I've only seen 1 or 2 in 45 minutes. How can I make this work?

Laura: I'm so pleased that you tried conferring about students' free choice books the day after we talked. I know from my own experiences that it's hard to focus—so feel encouraged that you've pinpointed the issue. Here are some suggestions you might try: (1) Be up front and tell the student you'll confer for about 10 minutes. (2) Based on your observations or on a student's request, pick one issue to discuss. Stick to one issue such as finding some problems the protagonist faced, adjusting predictions, or figuring out the meanings of new words using context clues. (3) Let the student know there's one to two minutes left. (4) Sum up high points. (5) If you need follow-up, tell the student you'll meet again soon. Let me know how things went.

Teacher: Sticking to one issue helped, as did telling the student we had about 10 minutes because I wanted to talk to others. One struggling reader will need many follow-ups. But it's better to focus and help her work on fluency than confusing her with too much info. I think I talked more than I listened. I'm going to work on that now. [Note that this back-and-forth dialoguing can help teachers pinpoint and think about issues on their own.]

Teacher: My students complain that I stopped reading aloud every day. It's true. But I have so much to cover. I need the time. Anyway, I'm not sure how reading aloud makes a difference. As you know, I have 40 minutes a day to teach reading to sixth graders. Besides, if I miss a few days with a novel, students don't remember the story and they lose interest. Do I really need to read aloud?

Laura: Having such a short time is frustrating as are the frequent disruptions in middle school schedules where you miss classes or lose half your time. I have the same experience in my eighth grade class when I read a novel and am forced to stop due to schedule changes. Here's how I've solved that problem: I read short stories, articles, legends, myths, and lots of poetry. I can fit in about two short novels from January through April as there are fewer schedule disruptions then. Start with poems and spend about five minutes reading aloud. Research on reading aloud shows it's a great way to introduce students to genres, literary language and style, and build vocabulary background knowledge about a topic. I have found that reading aloud is the best way to capture the imagination of struggling and reluctant readers, develop strong listeners, and nurture a personal reading life. Think about your students' reactions and ask them: Why is reading aloud important? You might use their comments and this e-mail to make a decision.

Teacher: I asked my students to anonymously write how they felt about reading aloud. One wrote, "I like it because you're doing it, not me." I laughed at that one. Most wrote that they loved hearing stories they couldn't read alone, and that it settled them into class. Two said that after I read a book, they got it from the library and tried to read it. I never thought of asking my students why they missed reading aloud. I think I need to do more of asking them things, like why they didn't do homework or why they seemed to be not listening. I'm trying to make reading aloud a priority. If I open the class with a read aloud every day, I know I'll do it.

Suggestions for Responding to Teachers' E-Mail Queries

Teachers who e-mail their concerns are fragile because they have confronted and shared a problem with an outsider. This is an ideal opportunity to build trust and honor the teachers' frank questions. When composing a response, be careful to do the following:

- Reply within two days. E-mail that results from a consulting commitment should always be high on your "to do" list.
- Honor teachers' concerns.
- Maintain a positive tone.
- Weave in your teaching experiences, providing a minimodel.
- Include research when appropriate.
- Suggest possible solutions, but don't tell teachers what to do.
- Offer choices.
- Encourage student input.

My goal is to ignite the reflective and questioning processes of the teacher, placing responsibility for thinking and deciding on him or her. If I make the decisions, then I disenfranchise instead of empower the teacher.

From Staff Development to Professional Study

As I rethought and revised the traditional inservice model, I realized that the term *staff development* did not adequately describe lifelong, self-directed learning. So I turned to Webster to confirm my hunch. Sure enough, one of Webster's definitions for development is "an event or happening." The words *staff development* imply a single experience such as an authority on a topic arriving at a school, delivering information, and departing. Constructivists such as Gordon Wells (1986), Donald Graves (1994), and Ellin Keene and Susan Zimmermann (1998) agree that learning is not an event, but a process, during which learners reinvent, reorganize, and construct knowledge through active learning and by linking new information to what they already know. The research on staff development by Bruce Joyce and Beverly Showers (1983) also supports the constructivist view of ongoing teacher training, showing how inquiry projects, study sessions, and the selection of professional readings can create growth and change in schools.

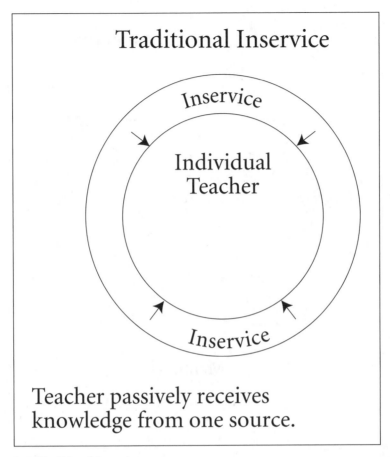

Figure 1–1. Traditional Inservice

The implications of the term *professional study* better describe the kind of lifelong learning I hope teachers and administrators will embrace. Most importantly, these words recognize teachers as professionals who study to keep abreast of research in their field. Webster's definition of *study* as "the act or process of applying the mind in order to acquire knowledge as by reading, investigating, etc." supports the contructivist theory of learning. The following diagram that I created illustrates how the rich elements woven into the patterns of professional study invite teachers to do, talk, and reflect in order to construct a theory of learning based on many experiences rather than asking teachers to accept a theory delivered in an inservice lecture (see Figures 1–1 and 1–2).

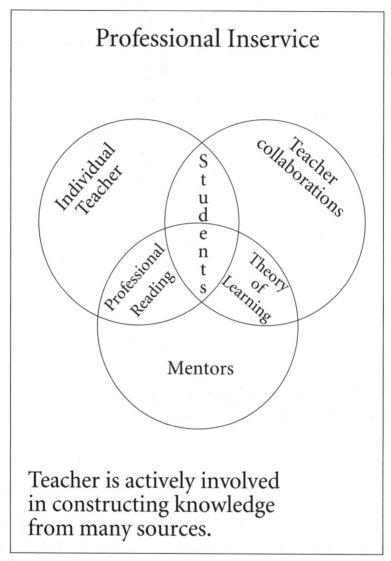

Professional Inservice

Individual Teacher

Teacher collaborations

Students

Professional Reading

Theory of Learning

Mentors

Teacher is actively involved in constructing knowledge from many sources.

Figure 1–2. Professional Study

Closing Thoughts

I have noticed that soon after a school community agrees to study and grow, teachers feel pressure from administrators to move forward at the speed of light, as if change were a wizard waving a wand and shouting, "Poof!", instantly allowing new teaching theories and practices to fall neatly into place. Whether perceived or real, such a fantasy is destructive, nurturing anger and frustration in the minds and souls of teachers. Pressure from administrators or from teachers' desire to change quickly is in opposition with the goals of professional study, which recognize that change can occur when there is administrative support and time to read, reflect, and move forward.

At Keister, Ann Conners and I discussed teacher frustration levels each time I visited, working to maintain a slow, comfortable pace. Our awareness of teacher anxiety issues and our commitment to watch for signs of stress enabled both of us to troubleshoot when necessary.

At the close of that first year, I had more invitations than I could accept because study-group sessions responded to teachers' requests for support, and there were no formal, high-pressure goals that teachers had to meet. It was a year of exploring ideas together and getting to know one another. Ann and I noticed that, more and more, lunchroom conversations centered around reading and writing and how a specific strategy helped a child or needed refining. During daily visits to classrooms, Ann Conners and Joe Nicholas observed teachers using chart paper to record reading and writing minilessons. Teachers provided time for students to practice strategies in class with books and their own writing.

Instead of pushing for instant changeovers, reflect on the advice Anne Morrow Lindbergh offers in the first chapter of her book *Gift from the Sea* (1983), called "The Beach." The beach, a metaphor for abandoning the hurried pace of our lives and stopping to savor experiences, links us to our "sea"—the school community. We should receive the "gifts" of our profession by observing children, collaborating and exchanging ideas with colleagues, and exploring the meanings each gift holds.

> The sea does not reward those who are too anxious, too greedy, or too impatient. To dig for treasures shows not only impatience and greed, but lack of faith. Patience, patience, patience, is what the sea teaches. Patience and faith. One should lie empty, open, choiceless as a beach—waiting for a gift from the sea. (17)

2

A Model for Professional Study

As I rummage through my mind, searching for experiences that led me to redefine traditional staff development, my memory reclaims an event at a middle school that occurred during my first outside consulting position. That experience taught me that forcing change reaps negative results.

At the start of my fourth year at that school, the principal called me into her office. Pleased that more teachers requested I team with them than I had time to support, she asked me to do her a favor. An eighth-grade reading-writing workshop teacher was on a probationary plan of improvement. Because the principal liked this teacher, believed in her potential, and did not want to ask her to leave at the end of the year, she implored me to work with her. At the principal's request, the teacher reluctantly consented to talk to me twice a week.

Today, I would have rejected this request, knowing, as John Goodlad (Stone 1999) points out, that change can not be imposed from the outside. At that point, my lack of experience and the imploring tone of the principal allowed me to agree.

Interested in drama, this teacher performed in many area theaters. My plan was to hook her by sharing and discussing several collections of plays. Over several weeks we read and discussed *Center Stage*, a group of one-act plays for teenage readers and actors, edited by Donald Gallo (1990). I found myself looking forward to these meetings, which soon transformed into dramatic readings, with each of us taking several parts.

After several weeks I asked this teacher to select some plays for her students to read and discuss, pointing out, "If the students can think, feel, and talk like their characters, then they are figuring out what kind of people they're portraying." My goal was to move students into active participation, studying characters' words, actions, and reactions, and gently move them away from fill-in-the-blank sheets and copying notes from the chalkboard. It didn't work. The teacher wanted no part of ruining a comfortable routine or creating a noisy classroom in which the outcomes of lessons wouldn't be clear or predictable.

Depression enveloped me, for I had invested in a relationship, had grown fond of this teacher, but was unable to link what she and I were doing to her students. I believed that I had failed the teacher, myself, and the principal.

At the end of the year, the teacher left; she found a position outside of teaching. Finally, after nursing my hurt for several months, I accepted that it was okay for her to *not* want to change. The problem here was with me and the principal, because we were dictating change in an unreasonably short span of time.

That year, I experienced an epiphany, a moment of truth, that shaped the professional learning model I was constructing and one I continue to revise. The following three elements support teachers as they digest new ideas and revise their thinking.

1. Plans of improvement and lists of changes teachers must accomplish can work only if the teacher understands the purpose of improving.

2. Teachers must desire change if it is to occur.

3. Support for teachers embarking on a journey that examines their present practices and introduces new, research-based ideas must be available over a period of several years.

As I reread the above list, a saying I heard often during my teen years reverberated in my mind; I had reviled it then, but now it made good sense: *You can lead a horse to water, but you can't make him drink.*

Integration Is Key

This professional model views schools as centers of inquiry, where teachers and administrators pose questions, pinpoint problems, study, reflect, and collaborate to discover possible answers. It is both dynamic and flexible, responding to and integrating into the study process the diverse needs of faculty and administrators. Therefore, as schools explore the model's beliefs, they will adapt its guidelines to meet their specific needs. And these needs will differ as the school community grows through study and with support networks.

Benefits of Posing Questions

Posing questions, as one teacher pointed out, "is the kindest way to spotlight issues and problems." The process can lead to inquiry, constructive learning, and problem solving. The questions that follow, posed by middle school reading-writing teachers during study-group sessions, highlight teachers' varied needs.

- What is a balanced reading program?
- How do I assess strategies?
- What are minilessons?
- How do I plan minilessons?
- How can I give students choices in reading?
- What do I put in the narratives that go with report cards?
- Who pays for the books we study?
- How do I balance choice and directed writing?
- Are there reading and writing strategies that I must teach?
- How can I shorten my conferences?
- How do I group students for reading?
- What do I do with students who can't read the class novel?
- How do I teach reading to this age group?

Setting priorities for professional study through consensus building requires administrative support. In this instance, team leaders helped teachers prioritize questions and decide which ones everyone wanted to study and which ones small groups would tackle.

Posing questions also highlighted a need to quickly find ways to support first-year teachers unfamiliar with strategies such as minilessons, grouping, and teaching reading. The principal instituted a peer-mentoring program for these new teachers, a program that prevented the escalation of frustration and low self-esteem.

Include Teachers in the Planning Process

When teachers have input into setting their study agenda, organizing support networks, and hiring an outside consultant, they are more likely to invest the time needed for ongoing professional learning. However—and John

Goodlad (Tell 1999) supports this belief—it's the school's responsibility to help teachers find the time to accomplish this.

Here are some ways to include teachers in the process:

- *Surveys:* Developed from questions teachers and administrators raise, surveys bring teachers into the planning process, show respect for their ideas, and can build trust and community as long as teachers remain an integral part of the planning process (see Appendix B).

- *Interviews:* Grade-level or team leaders question a consultant about his or her experience, knowledge base, theory of learning, and coaching strategies. Teachers bring the results of these interactions to the entire faculty and make a recommendation to the principal.

- *A Study-Group Session:* Scheduled by the principal and led by the consultant who has made a long-term commitment to the school, the study group closes with a question-and-answer period that enables teachers and the consultant to decide if the match will work.

I've participated in all three strategies. Surveys work well when I'm traveling by airplane to a school district several times and am not close enough to make an extra visit. The interview and a study-group session that reserves time for teachers to raise concerns are both effective ways for teachers and the consultant to get to know one another. I find that when principals encourage teachers to work in pairs or groups to raise questions prior to my visit, it improves the quality and quantity of their queries. Here are some frequently posed questions:

- Is your relationship with teachers confidential?
- How will you determine what we study?
- Do teachers have to accept invitations?
- Can you explain your theory of how children learn to read?
- Can you show us how to organize and manage a workshop?
- How much extra reading and work will we have to do?
- What literacy areas can you support us in?
- What happens if we don't extend an invitation?
- Do we have to complete all the reading assignments?

Provide Ample Time

Finding time to learn, grow, exchange ideas, and process information during the school day is crucial to the success of professional study (Churchill 1996).

Churchill and her colleagues met during a common, weekly lunch period, but not all schools have built-in common meeting times for teachers.

Principals who regularly hold three to four monthly faculty meetings can reserve one to two a month for professional study. Some principals gain time for study by handing teachers administrative notes to read several days prior to a meeting and dispensing with scheduling and reporting details quickly.

Accept Diverse Needs of Teachers

A primary goal of administrators is to honor the differences in experience and background knowledge among faculty, help teachers understand and accept that it's okay to be where they are, and through professional study and support networks gently nudge them forward. It is important in professional study to meet teachers' diverse needs.

Support Continual Follow-Up and Feedback

Since follow-up needs differ in each school, the principal, with teacher input, forms and annually evaluates ever-evolving support networks that address the needs of teachers in his or her school community. At Powhatan, the independent elementary school in Boyce, Virginia, where I teach and coach, the faculty reviewed the peer-evaluation program (see Chapter 7) at the end of the first year. One major pitfall was that the amount of time teachers committed to observing and meeting with peers varied greatly, even though dollars were set aside for substitutes to cover their classes. Teachers recommended that a group suggest a time line that the entire staff could review and edit. Periodic review identifies areas that need thought and revision. Without constant revision, a program's effectiveness can diminish and eventually cease to exist.

Develop Trust and Community

Shared decision making and shared learning empowers teachers and administrators to develop common goals and a theory of learning that can benefit all constituents in their school community. At Quarles Elementary School in Winchester, Virginia, most kindergarten and first-grade teachers voted to study guided reading and integrating word study into their language arts program. Near the end of the class, one kindergarten teacher told Quarles principal Nancy Lee that her theory of learning had shifted from a developmental stance, in which she never introduced anything new unless children showed they were ready, to recognizing that Vygotsky's (1978) "zone of proximal learning" allowed her to stretch children's potential through modeling, thinking aloud, and flexible reading groups.

Invite Teachers to Apply New Ideas and Share Strategies

All year long, Nancy Lee builds a safe environment at Quarles Elementary School. She not only encourages teachers to try the new strategies they are learning with me, but she also tells them, "It's okay if things don't work. I don't expect them to work quickly. What I'm hoping for is that you brainstorm ways to revise a strategy and dialogue with another teacher, me, or Laura."

Sharing teaching practices at Quarles occurs at team and faculty meetings, during study groups, and through informal chats among teachers at lunch, recess, and before school starts. Talk clarifies issues, enabling teachers to hear how colleagues use reading and writing centers, small-group mini-lessons, or dynamic grouping for guided reading. Talk might also entice a teacher to try a new idea.

Encourage Teachers to Reflect and Self-Evaluate

When administrators are visible in classrooms and engage teachers in reflective talk about students and/or a specific lesson, they can create a climate that values and fosters reflection and self-evaluation.

Administrators can help teachers find a balance between covering topics—or what often becomes a march through the curriculum, a pattern that discourages reflection and evaluation—and watching and thinking about students. By reflecting on observations, teachers can determine whether students understand how to plan, draft, and revise their writing, or how to set up science experiments that showcase their knowledge of a topic, or how to use context clues to figure out a word's meaning (Powers 1996; Watson 1987).

Ask Administrators to Participate Fully

Administrators who join professional study groups continue to develop as instructional leaders and build trust and community as they take on the tasks of teaching. As an outside consultant and as the professional study leader at Powhatan, I require administrators to attend study sessions and complete assignments. "Full participation," Ann Conners points out, "enables me to understand the process as I teach and monitor a group; it illustrates my dedication to learning by doing, [to] teaching, [to] teachers, and [to] children." If administrators can't make this commitment, then I won't consult.

Encourage Administrators to Support and Celebrate Staff Efforts

When my son, Evan, became the assistant principal of Warren County Middle School, in Front Royal, Virginia, he wrote this in his journal:

> I've taught for six years with occasional verbal feedback from administrators plus two annual evaluations. What I hungered for, especially during my first two years, was the feeling that someone was noticing the home visits I made, the extra time I was giving to struggling readers and writers. Once, a principal wrote me a note, complimenting the progress students made as a result of a before school, five-morning-a-week reading class. I kept the note in my desk, and every time I felt discouraged, reread it. My goal as an administrator is to be in classrooms, talk to teachers, and write notes that celebrate their work.

The administrator for five hundred students and twenty sixth-grade teachers, Evan made it a priority to briefly visit every teacher's room each day, spend quality time in six classrooms each week, and write a follow-up note to the six teachers. From regular classroom visits, follow-up chats, and personal notes that spotlighted what worked well, Evan relayed the message that he cared about teachers and students. If a teacher was struggling with discipline or with getting students actively involved in learning, Evan could initiate a nurturing conversation and suggest the teacher partner with a peer who could provide support. To be supportive and create a group of self-directed learners required Evan to be knowledgeable about students, teachers, and teachers' teaching practices and problems.

Teachers as Self-Directed Learners

In my role as consultant, in which I facilitate study groups and coach teachers, my goal is to develop self-directed learners who can continue growing without me. I've achieved success when I'm out of a job!

Teachers have helped me compile a list of the characteristics of self-directed learners.

Characteristics of Self-Directed Learners

- They are creative and imaginative.
- They take risks.
- They are confident.
- They are curious.
- They can focus and concentrate.
- They are knowledgeable in the teaching discipline.

- They are enthusiastic.
- They are motivated to learn and improve students' learning.
- They posess a philosophy of learning.
- They're organized.
- They manage time well.
- They are decision makers.
- They can self-evaluate and reflect.
- They set reasonable goals.
- They are responsive to others.
- They listen.

Though the list is daunting, the follow-up component of professional study can enhance and develop these traits. In a school that has ongoing follow-up for teachers, there is a support network teachers can count on to help them through the changes they are making. A support system draws from resource teachers, administrators, master teachers, district staff developers, and outside consultants. Follow-up provides continuous scaffolding for teachers as they learn and implement new, research-based strategies, and clarify and refine old and new ideas. Ultimately, support systems play a key role in changing a school's culture from isolation to collaboration. The end result? Students' learning improves.

Professional Study Options

Teachers can study and learn together as an entire faculty or in groups organized by grade levels, subjects, or topics. Professional study that investigates teachers' and administrators' inquiries can include the following elements:

- Study groups that replace faculty meetings or common planning times, which must be organized so teachers do not feel they are being coerced into changing. Therefore, a primary goal of administrators is to *invite teachers to learn,* not change, for through study with colleagues, teachers resistant to trying new strategies often change their stance when they gain background knowledge. In addition, when these study groups offer choice of topics and professional reading as well as allow teachers to set their own agendas, members feel empowered. Master or experienced teachers and/or an outside consultant can facilitate these sessions. Administrators are participants.

- Peer-mentoring programs for new teachers and those new to a school.
- Teacher-organized study groups that meet before or after school. These are voluntary.
- Peer coaching or coaching by an outside consultant, for which an invitation is extended to a teacher.
- A graduate or continuing-education class designed to respond to the specific needs of teachers attending.
- Follow-up networks that pair beginning teachers and experienced teachers new to a school with a colleague familiar with the school's culture. Partnerships can be formal peer-mentoring programs or informal pairings. The goal of follow-up networks is to help teachers acclimate to a school's culture and administrative tasks.
- Peer evaluation in which a teacher sets goals and a peer evaluator supports and guides the teacher all year.

Support Networks in Two Public Schools

Support networks are systems a school develops that help beginning teachers and experienced teachers new to a school adjust to a school's culture, administrative requirements, and expectations. These networks also invite all teachers to learn together as well as evaluate curriculum and teaching practices. I recommend that schools embarking on professional study consider constructing a peer-partnership program (see Chapter 4) and study groups (see Chapter 6), for they are inexpensive and easy to manage.

Support systems are works in progress, journeys without endings. Principals can develop effective networks for their faculty by using teacher evaluations and feedback from surveys and discussions to continually assess and revise new and existing scaffolding systems.

Robinson Elementary

Jane Gaidos, principal of W. W. Robinson Elementary School in Woodstock, Virginia, has begun a professional study program along with faculty networks. Interested in bringing word study to the primary grades, Jane invited one teacher each in kindergarten through fourth grade to take a three-credit class on word study at the University of Virginia. Because *Words Their Way* (Bear et al. 1996) was the text for that class, Jane purchased enough copies for all of her teachers. Trained teachers volunteered to be peer coaches for colleagues and could obtain release time to work with team members during teaching and planning periods. Teaching assistants and substitutes covered coaches' classes whenever they were working with colleagues. At team meetings, teachers debriefed, trading successes and brainstorming suggestions for coping with difficulties.

To provide all teachers with a strong overview of word study, Jane invited Dr. Phyllis Coulter, an expert on word study who teaches at Eastern Mennonite University in Harrisonburg, Virginia, to work with the faculty for a full day prior to the start of school. "We need Phyllis," Jane told me, "to inspire teachers and to provide common background information and hands-on experiences. She's a college professor who constantly works in teachers' classrooms." Following that, I will work with sixteen kindergarten and first-grade teachers at Robinson on guided reading and writing workshop, and Jane will help them form a teacher support network so they can receive guidance from Jane or a colleague.

Keister Elementary

For five years, Ann Conners has made teacher support networks a priority at Keister Elementary School. "I know that growth and change require ongoing support," Ann tells me. We both agree that a varied, in-school support network mines the expertise of teachers and builds self-esteem, as long as administrators provide the time to meet without overextending and frustrating teachers.

On Mondays, Ann requires that her teachers spend one hour after school for a faculty meeting, support groups, or special committees such as Child Study and Literacy and Technology. At Keister, this reserved time is flexible. For example, Keister teachers who work on Tuesday afternoons in a monthly study group with me have the choice to miss school support-group or faculty meetings on Mondays. "By the second year," Ann notes, "teachers were so invested in growth and change that most did not miss any meetings."

At the end of each school year, Ann Conners, her assistant principal, Joe Nicholas, and I have a breakfast meeting at my house to review the year, discuss teacher evaluations of professional study, and evaluate their suggestions for the next school year. Using teacher feedback that Ann and Joe have logged all year, we explore ways to improve old networks and suggest new ones to bring before the faculty. The networks that follow reveal the commitment that administrators and faculty have to helping one another. Within those networks, everyone has an important role.

Instructional team leaders   Appointed by the principal from a pool of volunteers, these are experienced teachers who poll their team to set the agenda for weekly meetings. At meetings, teachers share ideas, discuss curriculum, and ask the group to help them with specific students. Twice each month, instructional team leaders meet as a group to discuss curriculum and share ideas. They can serve as long as they like— one year or five years—and they receive an extra stipend.

Peer mentors or coaches   Master teachers and less-experienced teachers with expertise in specific areas, such as computers, flexible grouping, or writing to learn in mathematics, pair with first-year teachers and teachers new to Keister. They also collaborate with more-experienced colleagues who request assistance while implementing a new strategy. In grades K through 5, there is at least one master teacher to whom others can turn for support with planning lessons, refining teaching strategies, dealing with behavior issues, and completing clerical work. Teachers can meet during common planning periods, lunch, recess, or before the school day starts.

Resource teachers   Specialists in reading, English as a second language, computers, special education, and guidance collaborate with classroom teachers to provide positive learning experiences for mainstreamed students. These specialists chat with teachers during lunch and/or planning periods or before children arrive in the morning.

Literacy committee   This group consists of teachers and parents. Though their primary purpose is to plan the Title I budget and support-group meetings that focus on Title I students, teachers in this group frequently address faculty-raised issues that relate to reading and writing across the curriculum.

Administrators   A primary goal of Ann Conners and Joe Nicholas is to be instructional leaders so they can support teachers by responding to questions, sending them helpful professional materials, and teaming with them to plan lessons. They read professional journals and books and take graduate classes during the summer in reading-writing workshops, word study, assessment, and evaluation. Both participate, as members, in teacher-organized support groups, and both attend all study groups I facilitate. What Ann asks of teachers she does herself. When Ann invited all primary teachers to become proficient in taking and interpreting running records, Ann learned with her faculty. "I wanted to experience the process so I would understand how much time teachers needed to learn it," Ann told me. "I also wanted to be able to help teachers interpret running records."

Outside consultant   Between September and June, I spend one Tuesday a month at Keister. After two years of invitations, at the request of teachers, I have concentrated on two grade levels a year. One week prior to my visit, teachers create my schedule and fax me letters that guide my planning. I alternate grades, so in September, I'll visit all the fourth-grade classes; in October, all the fifth-grade classes.

During my visits, I team teach, present a model lesson, or observe. For one hour after school, teachers from both grade levels join a study-group session on a topic the majority of teachers in the group have selected. Kindergarten and first-grade teachers chose guided reading; second- and third-grade teachers studied guided reading and writing workshop; fourth- and fifth-grade teachers focused on record keeping that encouraged reflecting about struggling readers, flexible grouping, and reading workshop.

High on my agenda as an outside consultant is to strengthen ongoing professional study by encouraging teachers to revisit, evaluate, and revise existing support systems; add networks; and take charge of their education. During years three to five at Keister, I worked with two different grade levels each year, starting with kindergarten and first grade. Teachers and I framed a study-group agenda around their needs. For the rest of the faculty, teacher-organized study-groups became an important way to study, share, and support one another. Instead of adding more study-group sessions, Ann changed the organization of faculty meetings from administrative talk to teachers exchanging ideas, professional articles, and state and national conference experiences.

Support activities at Keister include the following:

Teacher-organized study groups   Each year, teachers who want to learn together brainstorm a list of topics they would like to study. If the list is too long, then teachers prioritize topics, narrowing the choices down to six or seven. Groups meet on at least six Mondays during the school year, share personal knowledge and experiences, and read and discuss professional articles and books on topics such as portfolio assessment, struggling readers, choosing trade books, grouping for instruction, and writing in the content areas. These study groups are in addition to ones led by an outside consultant.

Informal lunch meetings   Resource and classroom teachers prize this time that Ann has set aside for them. Ann, Joe, and teaching assistants cover the students' cafeteria during all scheduled lunch seatings, allowing grade teams to have thirty minutes each day to eat and chat in a faculty lunchroom. Here, teachers socialize, exchange projects and strategies, and trade stories about children.

Consultant-facilitated study groups   These one-hour meetings open with me celebrating a minilesson, guided-reading group, writing conference—something I observed in each class I attended. Next, teachers share a strategy they tried during the weeks between my visit; they bring minilesson charts and student work, which we all read and discuss. The study group closes with a discussion of the chapter in a book and/or the article we've read and the questions teachers pose.

Funding Professional Study

Some administrators tell teachers, "We don't have the money for a professional study program." This statement has more to do with a principal's theory of how people learn than with the availability of dollars.

Jane Gaidos, principal of W. W. Robinson Elementary School, told me during a planning session, "I can't afford *not* to provide my staff with a meaningful study program. How principals spend money is a matter of priorities." To the staff development money in her school budget, Jane added profits from school pictures and the soda and snack machines. Dollars for classroom libraries and trade books for the curriculum came from fund-raisers sponsored by the parent organization. In one year, parents raised ten thousand dollars for books for children and promised to continue raising money for books annually. Another way that Jane raised money was to apply for a grant from money her school district received from the federal government's Title VI literacy fund. Each year, the school district receives Title VI dollars, and teachers can apply for Title VI grants as long as the proposal relates to literacy issues. To purchase trade books and leveled titles for guided reading for kindergarten through grade two, Jane received a grant for six thousand dollars. This funding enabled Jane to reroute dollars set aside for books in those grades toward professional study with an outside consultant.

Ann Conners, like Jane Gaidos, increased the dollars designated for staff development with profits from snack and soda machines and school pictures. In addition, she added Title I and Head Start Staff Development funds to her budget and asked these teachers to participate in study groups I led. She also asked them to invite me into their classrooms to support their teaching.

Now that Virginia has adopted uniform standards of learning, called SOLs, the state provides each school district with staff development money to improve teaching practices and students' performance on SOL tests. Both Jane and Ann benefited from extra staff development money given by Virginia and divided among schools in each district.

Professional Study on a Tight Budget

When Warren County appointed my son, Evan, to be principal of Warren County Junior High, a new school for eighth and ninth graders, he posed the following questions to himself and to me because he wanted to spend the limited dollars in his budget wisely.

- How can I use my staff development dollars to strengthen faculty?
- During the hiring process, how can I help teachers invest in a professional study plan?
- What kind of survey should I develop that identifies teachers' strengths, needs, conferences they'd like to attend, and professional books and magazines they'd like in the library?

Evan also asked me to read this short journal entry:

I don't think change will occur if I blow my budget on one or two presentations by outside consultants. There's no money in this year's budget to have someone here on a regular basis, and second, I want a plan that invites administrators, teachers, parents, and students to learn and progress through communication, an exchange of ideas, and study.

We discussed professional study that improves teacher performance and students' learning, and Evan emphasized these points: "I want teachers to be able to evaluate the professional study program and to develop performance-based methods of evaluating students' progress."

We developed a base plan in four phases. The purpose of having phases is to allow ample opportunity to self-evaluate and improve each element, moving at a rate that supports rather than frustrates teachers. When they felt ready, groups adopted parts of or all of new phases. Teachers Evan considered hiring read the plan, offered suggestions, and completed a survey (see Appendix B). Those who committed to making the program work joined the faculty. Following are the four phases in the original plan, which will be revised annually through anonymously written feedback.

Phase 1

- Teachers, department chairs, and administrators will develop a peer-partner and peer-coaching program.
- Department chairs will identify teachers who have demonstrated practices worthy of sharing.
- The principal and/or one of his assistants will attend these meetings and follow up and write commendations as well as offer support for teachers.

- Once each month, during departmental meetings, a teacher will demonstrate a teaching strategy or technique by:
  a. explaining the purposes of the strategy/technique
  b. actively involving others in the "doing"
  c. providing a handout that summarizes the process
  d. closing the session with a question/answer period
  e. discussing, after teachers have had two weeks to try the strategy, what worked and raising questions about any kinks

Evan told me that many experienced teachers he interviewed had participated in departmental meetings that focused on schedules and completing forms rather than on study. Of the more than forty teachers interviewed, none had ever been asked to reflect on and share their expertise with colleagues. They liked these changes; but, Evan observed, "I believe teachers will need even more than the one year I envisioned to feel comfortable with phase one."

Phase 2

- Department heads and a member of their team will attend at least one conference or workshop per year in their subject area.
- Attendees will bring back two to three ideas to share with colleagues at departmental meetings. The method of sharing, whenever possible, will follow the process in phase 1.
- The school librarian, department chair, and principals will work together to identify a minimum of four professional articles a year for teachers to read and discuss. Discussions will focus on how each article applies to their teaching. Teachers will be encouraged to suggest professional books and articles.
- Teachers will be encouraged to implement one idea from an article. The department chair and the principals will be responsible for follow-up and support, helping teachers become risk takers and learners.

Phase 3

- Teachers, department chairs, and administrators will consider establishing cross-discipline and cross-grade study groups. These will not be schoolwide, but among groups who wish to study together.

Phase 4

- Decisions on obtaining outside consultants for departments will be made by principals, teachers, and department chairs.

- Outside consultants will be brought in periodically to facilitate study groups or provide several short hands-on sessions.
- Administrators will attend all workshops as well as encourage and support teachers' efforts.

Tight budgets for professional study force principals and teachers to be more creative in designing professional study programs. Here are some suggestions:

- Provide teachers with professional materials from public and university libraries. Teachers will have to share these resources, but it is possible to develop a sign-out system that allows many teachers to read the same article or chapter from a book before a study group convenes.
- Use some substitute funding for teachers to spend the day in exemplary schools and learn by observing and dialoguing with another professional.
- Invite area experts or those in a school district with expertise to volunteer time to meet and converse with teachers.
- Ask parents and retired teachers with expertise to volunteer some of their time.
- Start with teachers learning to become expert observers of students, then bringing their observations and work samples to a study group for discussion.
- Work with an area business and ask it to support a professional study project. Before approaching a business, have a written plan ready that details materials needed, includes an outline of what teachers plan to do, and provides a list of how the project benefits teachers, students, and administrators.

Closing Thoughts

A move from the traditional staff development model to professional study requires leadership and commitment from the principal and other administrators in a school district. Quite often, I receive a telephone call from a principal asking me to "get teachers to do reading and writing workshop" or developmental word study or guided reading or raise standardized test scores in one day or one morning. At first, I'd have closed the door and refused to come. Now, I request a meeting with the principal and other school administrators. My goal? To try to convince them that time and support and their involvement alongside teachers foster change.

Here is a checklist of questions administrators can periodically review as they move their staff toward professional study.

_____To continuously grow and revise my theory of how children learn, do I fully participate in study groups and read professional materials?

_____To pace the rate of change, do I suggest teachers choose one strategy to implement—a strategy they feel will benefit students' literacy?

_____To enable teachers to risk trying new ideas, do I provide follow-up and support?

_____To encourage teachers to learn from their mistakes, do I recognize that the time needed to introduce, reflect on, and revise a strategy differs for each teacher?

_____To help teachers exchange ideas and learn from one another, have I provided meeting times during the regular school schedule?

In a conversation with Carol Tell in the May 1999 issue of *Educational Leadership,* John Goodlad said that in his lifetime, he would like to lift teaching "into a profession of high demand and high expectation. A profession in which you always have to be learning more" (19). Here is a checklist of questions teachers can periodically review while they collaborate and learn:

_____Are we taking the time to listen to all teachers' inquiries and concerns?

_____Have we worked for consensus on when to meet and what to study?

_____Can we convince the school to purchase professional books?

_____How can we support one another in our classrooms?

_____How can we create a climate in which it's okay for teachers to report mistakes and learn from them?

_____Have we gathered evidence that shows our study is improving the literacy of children we teach?

_____Do we ask students to evaluate new strategies we've tried?

_____Do we remain focused on our goals?

3

Creating a Climate for Change

In 1982 two books were published that deepened my connection to the writing process: *Learning by Teaching* by Donald Murray and *Writing: Teachers and Children at Work* by Donald Graves. That year I invited Carol Chapman, second-grade teacher at Powhatan School, to read and discuss these books with me. Carol, a nurturing, sensitive teacher, feared writing. "When someone says 'write,' I can still feel the churning in my stomach," Carol told me. "I hated and feared writing all through school, and I know I don't do enough writing with my students. But I don't know what to do, and I don't want to transmit my fears."

Those books—and another four years later, Lucy Calkins' *The Art of Teaching Writing* (1986)—changed Carol forever. With the consent of the school's head, Carol plunged her second graders into writing workshop. Imprinted in my memory is the afternoon Carol rushed across the library to my classroom. It was about ten minutes before dismissal. My sixth graders were cleaning up and packing books. Out of breath, Carol grabbed my hand and pulled me toward her room. "You've got to see this," she said. "They [her students] refuse to stop writing." Under desks, on the floor, and at tables, sixteen second graders worked alone, in pairs, or in small groups. Some wrote; some shared. "We don't want to go home yet," one explained. "We have to write." Only after Carol promised to start the next day with workshop did the class agree to get ready to ride the school buses home.

Professional study at Powhatan began with two teachers reading, talking, and working together to develop writing workshops in their classrooms or bring process writing to history, math, and science. By the time Lucy Calkins published her book, more than half the teachers at Powhatan were reading about process writing and organizing writing workshops. To help parents break with their traditions and understand the benefits of writing workshop, I facilitated several evening sessions. The school started a professional library and purchased books teachers and our librarian, Anne Wheeler, recommended.

When the writing workshop fever hit our school, no teacher was coerced into studying and changing. However, the constant, enthusiastic talk brought some reluctant teachers into workshop classrooms. Teachers carved out time for professional study from their schedules: early morning and after-school meetings, common planning periods, chats at recess, and occasionally some time after weekly faculty meetings. In 1994, when John Lathrop became Head of Powhatan, he set aside one faculty meeting a month for professional study. Some teachers still use their own time. However, not everyone can give up extra time. By integrating study into the school schedule, administrators can allow every teacher to grow.

The Principal's Role in Professional Study

For a school to construct a solid professional study foundation, the principal must be supportive. Many ongoing programs originate from a principal's desire to improve instruction and students' performance. At Quarles Elementary, Nancy Lee and her teachers invited me to facilitate a study group on guided reading with kindergarten and first-grade faculty. Within two weeks I learned that through assessments, teachers had identified forty kindergarten children who did not know their alphabet, had no concept of word, and experienced little to no storybook reading at home. Several did not know what a book was for. Attending to shared reading and collaborative story writing was difficult for these students because they lacked a sense of what stories are all about. Six to eight of these children were in each of the five kindergarten classes. The literacy story that follows illustrates how professional study enabled teachers and administrators to respond to children, alter and adjust teaching practices, help children progress, and utilize and develop the teaching talents of instructional assistants.

Nancy invited me to propose a program for these literacy-deprived children, a program we named Literacy Links. That night I returned to two books about family reading: *Read to Me: Raising Kids Who Love to Read* by Bernice E. Cullinan (1992) and *Family Storybook Reading* by Denny Taylor and Dorothy S. Strickland (1986). Passages from each book influenced the program I suggested.

Reading aloud contributes to a child's ability to read alone. This happens naturally for many children who sit on a parent's lap to listen and to watch the reader's finger move across the page pointing to the words as they are read. Gradually, over time, children make connections between the sounds of words and squiggles on the page. (Cullinan, 27)

Hug me, love me, and grow with me is the message that parents and children find hidden between the pages of the books that they share. Even the youngest of children can read this message and understand its meaning. Family storybook reading is a time when parents and children learn from one another as their lives come together in the stories that they read. (Taylor and Strickland, 111)

A Lap Reading Program: How One School Created a Climate for Change

Since at Quarles Elementary, each kindergarten class of twenty-two children has an instructional assistant, I suggested that the assistants simulate family storybook reading. Three days a week, three times a day, I wanted assistants to read, sitting close to four to five children; I believed that in small groups, laughter and talk about books would develop among these children a genuine interest in stories and their structure. We had years to make up, and my goal was for the children to associate warm, nurturing feelings with reading and sharing stories about books.

However, in order to free up teaching assistants, classroom teachers had to take on extra work. Kindergarten teachers agreed to pilot the plan for two months, assess children, and then decide whether to continue. The vote to continue was unanimous.

Instructional assistants and I formed a study group to practice building children's book and word knowledge once children showed enthusiasm for storybook reading. These women agreed to maintain detailed records of the books read and a prereading competency checklist for each child (see Appendix C). All kept observational notes that documented changes in children and/or behaviors they wanted to discuss as a group.

After teaching assistants launched the program, they met with me twice during the trial months, then every six weeks. Together, and with the classroom teachers they supported, these women exchanged experiences, celebrated successes, and read articles about emergent literacy that I offered them.

In April, the teaching assistants and I spoke to the Winchester School Board and celebrated the success of this program. Ninety percent of the children knew all their alphabet letters; more than 60 percent had mastered most letter-sound relationships. Six children had developed some sight words, and all the children could point to the front and back covers, title, and dedication pages. They knew that the words told the story. All had developed favorite books and asked for these to be read again and again. Frequently, children begged to be read to instead of working at centers or playing games during recess. Classroom teachers noted that, by April, all had begun to "pretend read" books during sustained silent reading. By the end of the school year, all had begun to predict and offer support for predictions while listening to a story.

Extending the Program to Summer School

Based on the data teaching assistants and I collected, I requested funds for a summer program to ensure that the children continued to progress. Thirty-four invitations were mailed to parents in May; thirty families accepted and their children attended the six-week program. Superintendent Glenn Burdick and Nikki Isherwood, Director of Instruction, released funds for a three-day-a-week, three-hour-a-day summer school. In May, three teaching assistants and I studied, reviewed student samples, and engaged in writing workshop and shared reading, the morning message, and other shared writing experiences. Again, they agreed to complete an observational note form as children read their stories, sitting in the author's chair, and we added another checklist of reading behaviors we hoped would develop through shared reading (see Appendix C).

Author's chair and a free-choice writing workshop were new to these children. Richard, the first youngster in Nancy Reedy's class to read his story from the author's chair, announced, "I'm so proud; I'm telling my mom and grandma I'm an author as soon as I get home." Quickly, all ten children in Nancy's class, through this experience, expressed their pride in "writing" stories and feeling special in the author's chair.

On the last day of the summer program, Nancy Reedy invited the school board, central office administrators, Nancy Lee, the children's parents, and me to a celebration of each child's progress. Every child received a certificate and a book of his or her own, and the teaching assistants read a statement honoring each child's growth.

Next year, when these children enter first grade, teaching assistants will continue lap reading with them, encouraging the children to retell books and imagine and share their own stories.

One Kindergartner's Story

Joan Norris, a teaching assistant at Quarles, told this story at one of our study sessions. Joshua (fictitious name), a boy in her kindergarten class who had never been read to before he arrived at school, always interrupted minilessons and shared reading by shouting phrases like, "I want to play," and "Let's go outside." In small-group work, Joshua would punch others, take their toys, and shout angrily, "I didn't do anything," if the teacher removed him for a time-out. Reluctant to come with Joan and three classmates for storybook reading, he chose to sit apart from the others, who nestled close to Joan on pillows in the hall outside the classroom. For two months, Joshua listened to three stories a day sitting apart from the group. Joan accepted his behavior and said nothing. "I knew I couldn't make him want to sit with us," she told us. "Inside, I knew he was confused and didn't trust me yet. Joshua needed time."

"The day Joshua asked if he could sit with me my heart leapt out of my chest. 'Sure,' I answered, trying to sound as casual as possible. He snuggled in close to me and helped turn the pages. On that day, he became part of our foursome and allowed himself to look at a book and make contact with me and other children."

"In March, Joshua showed me how he could read the words from a simple caption book. [Actually, he had memorized them.] That day, the teacher and I invited him to sit in the reader's chair and share the book with his classmates. He grinned the widest smile I'd ever seen when his classmates applauded."

Joan ended her story by passionately saying, "I know it was the nurturing and hearing stories that calmed him down. Back in the classroom, Joshua could relate to his teacher reading books, for he had discovered that books contain wonderful stories. Now he *wanted* to listen—he was able to listen—so he stopped disrupting."

Extending Support Networks

Near the end of the school year, three teaching assistants and Nancy Lee, Nikki Isherwood, and I appeared on Winchester Public Schools television to discuss the Literacy Links program. Our goal was to inform the community about the success of this intervention program. We planned to show the video at parent meetings and to other principals in order gain support to add similar programs in other Winchester schools and school districts.

The program closed with teaching assistant Nancy Reedy's statement that illustrates how much professional study affected the teaching lives and beliefs of these women:

> We feel that this program has started a relationship between children and books. Not every child can have a computer in their home, but every child can have access to books. Through this program, we have encouraged children to borrow books from the library, the classroom, from an older sister, brother, or friend. This program has encouraged us to put children on our laps and sit closely while reading stories that make us laugh and bring tears to our eyes. We snuggled with the children while reading and saw the difference this nurturing made. We accomplished much, for these children have come to love listening to and talking about stories and have favorites they beg to be read again and again. We believe that books will now always be an important part of their lives.

Setting the Stage for Professional Study

Before embarking on schoolwide professional study, administrators and teachers should ponder and discuss two questions: Where does knowledge about teaching and children come from? and Are some sources of knowledge more important than others? Wrestling with these questions can help learners recognize that knowledge in a school community comes from different sources: individual teachers and groups of teachers, administrators, students, parents, and mentors who can be authors of books and articles as well as experts in an area within or outside a school district. An explosion of ideas and energy for learning can occur when schools include the whole community in professional study.

Questions and Guidelines for Administrators to Consider

Effective administrators recognize that they shape the climate and culture within a school. I gave my son, Evan, the questions below when he became assistant principal of Warren County Middle School, cautioning him to revisit them periodically and use them as a barometer of the climate he was creating and to evaluate his leadership style.

- Do I dispense information or encourage independent thinking?
- Do I collaborate with teachers?
- Do I offer support for professional study?
- Do I model ongoing learning by sharing professional articles with staff?

- Do I join teachers in professional study ventures?
- How do I show respect for teachers' ideas?
- Am I a top-down or consensus-building person?

According to Evan, reflecting on these questions "kept me in touch with my teachers' feelings and helped me choose strategies that supported teachers." The following are the administrative strategies Evan developed during his year as assistant principal of Warren County Middle School—strategies that created a strong communication bridge between him and teachers, developed trust, and built community.

- Visit classrooms daily and chat with teachers to discover the kinds of support they need.
- Keep a calendar/planner with you when you visit classrooms, so you can note teachers' requests and follow up within twenty-four hours.
- Build consensus for instructional changes at faculty meetings and grade-level team meetings.
- Observe, informally, all teachers several times a year. Spend a full period.
- Attend as many team meetings as possible. Share articles and books you've read; purchase books for the school's professional library.
- Encourage teachers to invite you into their classrooms.
- Deliver paychecks to each teacher every month. Thank teachers for their commitment, and whenever possible, briefly point out progress with teaching, team building, classroom management, and student-teacher relationships.

The most difficult yet most important thing Evan learned during his first year as an administrator was "to put aside paperwork and do it after school, making teachers and students my top priority." Evan admitted that completing work during school hours was a temptation he had to fight hard to resist, but it was a fight he never regretted.

Assessing a School's Needs

A school reflects its principal's leadership style and educational beliefs. If the principal is a top-down person who makes all decisions about curriculum, books, teaching style, types of assessments, schedules, and so on, then it's almost impossible for teachers to be honest and open about assessing their needs, feelings, and hopes.

I am a careful school watcher in the many schools I visit. By taking in the outward trappings of a school, I can quickly assess what the principal values and what are his or her beliefs about how children learn. One teacher told me that she had just suspended group work in her sixth-grade class because students were shouting and did not quiet down after two warnings. Just when the students were silent and the teacher had begun to read aloud, the principal walked by the classroom. She popped into the class and complimented the teacher for maintaining silence. Aware that silence was valued at the school, the teacher felt that her reading-writing workshop continually ruffled the principal. If the principal passed by while forty students discussed books in their learning voices, she always told the teacher to quiet them down.

There are schools where children only learn in neat rows, complete skill worksheets, copy into notebooks information covering the chalkboard, and line up and march silently from class to class. Teachers rarely rise from their desks to circulate among students; instead of observing and supporting students, they're grading worksheets and controlling students' behavior with phrases like "Stop talking, Jamal" or "One more word, Lisa, and you're off to the principal's office." Tacked on bulletin boards are perfect scores on spelling and math tests or teacher-made displays. The principal remains in his office completing paperwork, leaving the day-to-day running of the school to his assistant. However, the principal's values and beliefs about how children learn are omnipresent.

Ann Conners' leadership style is a foil to the above scenario. Everywhere a visitor walks in Keister Elementary School, children's artwork and writing, collaborative murals, and data-retrieval charts decorate the halls. Desks are arranged in small communities: sometimes in pairs, other times in groups of three to five. Every classroom has a rug for shared learning experiences. Teachers constantly make the rounds, visiting students as they read and write. Children's writing, from brainstorming to published drafts, fill bulletin boards. Current minilessons are on the walls so students can use the information as they work. A list of student-generated behavior guidelines hangs in a prominent place. In the halls, teachers waiting with their classes chat quietly; children walk with a partner and occasionally whisper to one another or greet a visitor with a quiet "Hello." Whenever Ann doesn't have a scheduled meeting, she visits classrooms, reads aloud to children, meets with students to discuss books they're reading, and encourages students to write her letters, which she always answers.

Teachers acknowledge that Ann demands a lot from them and students. However, they love working at Keister because Ann builds consensus and collaborates with her staff in all professional study experiences.

No matter what a school's culture is like, I suggest teachers anonymously complete inquiry surveys to assess its needs. Posing questions allows teachers to express themselves without assigning blame, which in turn can escalate negative, unproductive feelings among colleagues and administrators.

Administrators can use the questions to reflect on teaching and learning practices in their schools and the values and beliefs that drive these practices. If a principal's values differ dramatically from what his or her faculty prizes, then it's time to talk about these issues and open the doors to collaboration and change.

I have identified seven areas schools should consider in their needs assessment. Under each heading I've included suggested questions that can be selected for a survey (see Appendix B). Select and add any questions that will pinpoint your school's needs. I use this key for administrators and teachers to rate each question: Never, Rarely, Sometimes, Most of the Time, Always. At the end of a survey, always provide space under the heading "Additional Questions" for queries the survey did not include. The following list details some of the questions schools might address in each assessment area.

School environment   Do bulletin boards celebrate students' work? Are the processes of reading and writing valued? Are classrooms silent? Do students collaborate to problem solve and learn? How do students walk through the halls? Are there cross-grade projects? Do students sit in rows? small groups? Are there classroom libraries?

District-level support and money   Does the district set aside money for professional study in each school's budget? Does the superintendent visit district schools? Does the district make decisions for teachers about the books they use?

Administrative support within a school   Is the principal visible? Does the principal participate with teachers in all professional study? Are faculty and/or team meetings used for professional study? Is the principal available to meet with teachers? Does the principal follow up on promises to support? Does the principal regularly visit and work in classrooms? Are decisions about curriculum collaborative? Does the principal listen and respond to teachers? Is the principal open to ideas suggested by teachers? by students? by parents?

Time   Is there time in the school day for pairs or groups of teachers to meet? Is there pressure to cover curriculum in a specific time period?

Consensus building and shared decisions   Does the principal poll teachers if a decision must be made between scheduled meetings? Is teachers' input valued? Do teachers collaborate with administrators on decisions that relate to professional study and curriculum?

Parent education   Do parents volunteer? Are parent volunteers trained to help in classrooms? Are parents educated about changes in curriculum? assessment? evaluation? teaching practices? Are parents invited to special programs?

Teachers and teaching   Do children learn to read at their instructional level? Do teachers use reading workshop? writing workshop? Do teachers attend two to three inservices a year? Does the school have peer mentors and peer partners? Do all teachers have opportunities to attend state and national conferences?

Are teachers vocal about their desire to change? Do teachers study together? Are some teachers vocal about maintaining the status quo? Are there support networks for new teachers? Does the school have a coaching or peer-mentoring system? Do teachers collaborate to plan lessons? Do teachers collaborate to discuss students? Do teachers share their resources? Do teachers respect differences in one another's teaching styles? Do teachers listen to one another? Do teachers build consensus among themselves? their students?

Moving Beyond the Needs Assessment

Answering these questions can reveal a school's culture and spotlight what's working, what's missing, and what needs revising. The following are some reasons that compel administrators and teachers to assess their school's environment and plan a professional study program.

- Students produce low test scores in reading, writing, or math.
- The central office decides that schools must change.
- The principal, after visiting schools, sees a need for change.
- Several teachers have begun a study group and others want to join. As a result, the need for ongoing study emerges.
- Teachers and instructional leaders, after attending a conference, taking a class, reading a book, and/or visiting other schools, lobby for change.
- A vocal group of parents expresses a need for changes.
- A new principal with different beliefs and leadership style highlights the need for change.
- An outside consultant observes a school, conducts a needs-assessment survey, and summarizes the results.

After Jane Gaidos completed her first year as principal of Robinson Elementary School in Woodstock, Virginia, she and her faculty assessed their needs. Students' performance on Virginia's Standards of Learning Tests in reading and writing had not met state standards. The low scores nudged Jane and grade-level teams to verbally assess their curriculum, support networks, and professional study programs. Together, they identified two areas for professional study: (1) reading instruction based on a consistent theory of how children learn to read, and (2) writing workshop.

Once schools decide that professional study and establishing support networks are primary goals, the next step is for administrators and teachers to collaborate and determine where to begin. Since test scores create so much negative publicity in community newspapers and among politicians, responding to them and effecting positive growth can help schools gain community support for continuing professional study.

Overcoming Teachers' Resistance to Change

Even with a consensus-building approach, the principals I've collaborated with recognize that some teachers, though they join a study support group, refuse to change. I have found that a principal's philosophy of how children learn determines the way he or she interacts with a teacher while negotiating revision of classroom practices.

I interviewed Nancy Lee, principal of Quarles Elementary School, and Bill Flora, assistant superintendent of instruction of Warren County public schools, to explore this challenging issue.

Negotiating Change: Interview with Nancy Lee

A classroom teacher and assistant principal for more than fifteen years, Nancy has been the principal at Quarles for seven years. Her experience has been in elementary schools. I met Nancy when she took a graduate class in reading that I was teaching.

Laura: Nancy, what is your philosophy of how children learn?

Nancy: I believe that teachers have to be flexible with their teaching styles. The content of the curriculum is a constant, but the way it's taught must vary with each child's needs and learning style. Watching kids is important and responding to their learning needs follows. Time—slowing down to support children who don't get it is crucial. It's difficult to progress when the foundation and key strategies are shaky or missing.

Laura: How do you stay in touch with the daily pressures your teachers experience as they try to individualize learning?

Nancy: I feel strongly that a principal doesn't know how a classroom teacher feels—frustrations, behavior problems, parent concerns, and the added pressure of Virginia's Standards of Learning with its rigorous testing program—unless she's in the classroom. That's why I teach one class each day—it might be reading or writing. The very least a principal must do is spend time in a teacher's room, observing and team teaching or guiding a small group.

Laura: Does your philosophy about how children learn connect to the way you interact with teachers who resist change?

Nancy: Definitely. You see, if a majority of a class is performing low on teacher and district assessments and on standardized tests, then I focus on that class. In my first meeting with the teacher I emphasize my concerns about children's performance and achievement.

Laura: Can you elaborate?

Nancy: After several classroom visits, the teacher and I meet and discuss students' performance and my observational notes. I introduce alternate teaching strategies and provide articles and books for the teacher to read. In addition to meeting with me, I ask the teacher to meet with our reading specialist and/or with you, our consultant.

Laura: How often do you meet at this point?

Nancy: Many meetings, as negotiating change takes time. What I've discovered over the years is that most teachers are willing to look at and discuss change, but [they're] not always willing to apply what they've read about in their classrooms.

Laura: How do you combat continued resistance?

Nancy: I'll ask the teacher to observe colleagues or send him to another school to observe several times. Sometimes, watching the model-in-action along with time to talk with a colleague enables a teacher to try a different strategy. During these conversations, I'm searching for ways to support the teacher. I always volunteer to help plan an innovative lesson.

Laura: Seems like you're investing a lot of time.

Nancy: Yes, but it's worth it if it works. To institute meaningful change and gain a deep understanding of a new teaching practice won't occur quickly. I might also ask the teacher's team leader to play a key role. Team leaders are expert teachers, and I'll arrange a coaching relationship if I believe it can effect change. [Nancy points out that her team leaders are very busy mentoring first-year teachers and faculty new to Quarles.]

Laura: But what do you do if a teacher still won't come on board?

Nancy: That's a sad point that I've reached several times in my career. Sometimes I ask a teacher if she'd like to move to another grade or another school with a philosophy more in tune with hers.

Constructing a Common Vision: Interview with Bill Flora

Bill Flora's experience has been in middle schools. A veteran teacher and principal, Bill has been in charge of instruction in Warren County for several years. Bill Flora has an unusually close relationship with all of his principals; he encourages them to communicate successes as well as imperfect days and is a supportive, sympathetic listener. At the request of principals, he works directly with teachers, helping them plan minilessons, interventions, and reasonable goals for themselves and students.

Laura: Bill, do you have a philosophy of how children learn?

Bill: Students arrive at school with different levels of readiness. It's the teacher's responsibility to discover where students are and engage them in classroom activities that meet individual needs. Students build on their successes and improve as a result of good teaching.

Laura: How do you communicate your philosophy to teachers and other administrators?

Bill: That's a crucial part of my job. At administrative meetings we discuss how children learn best and the kinds of instruction that foster growth and progress. We hire building-level administrators who are in harmony with these beliefs, and they maintain the vision at each school. A high priority among administrators is to find ways to help teachers continually reach for the vision.

Laura: Why do you spend most of the school day with teachers and principals in their buildings?

Bill: That's part of constructing a culture around my vision. The strong ties I establish with people can help me create change.

Laura: Can you explain how this works?

Bill: If teachers observe me interacting with principals, teachers, children, and learning from conversations with a school's staff, then I'm providing a model for communicating and learning among teachers. I believe that positive changes emerge from positive relationships between me, principals, and teachers.

Laura: Can you give an example?

Bill: If a principal asks me to help her coach a teacher who requires guidance, then I'm available. Prior to visiting the teacher's class, I meet with the teacher and listen to his concerns and feelings. After three to four observations that close with follow-up conversations, I negotiate strategies with the teacher that might include planning lessons together, team teaching, observing a more experienced peer. The principal, teacher, and I work together as we provide the scaffolding to effect change. The primary goal is to improve the ways children are learning.

Laura: What happens if after this investment of time and energy, the teacher still resists change?

Bill: The principal and I write a plan of assistance and the teacher has one year to meet the plan's goals or there will be no future contracts. I hope that day never arrives because it advertises the failure of our support networks. This step is hurtful to the children and to other faculty, as bad news spreads quickly and demoralizes all school-community members.

Ten Conditions That Contribute to Change

I hope politicians and administrators will stop searching for a remedy, a quick fix that will make scores soar and transform schools into places where all members are passionate about learning and thinking and all test scores are above average. Instead, I urge them to put slogans aside, assess their needs, and diligently work toward creating ten factors that indicate professional study is a vital part of their school's culture.

1. *Positive Tension and Discomfort:* Sparks fly when teachers explore new ideas because they generate conflicts while testing and measuring new information against what they already know and do. I'm delighted when teachers experience discomfort while risking change. Discomfort means they are questioning present teaching practices and searching for a clearer understanding of where they hope to travel.

2. *Personal Commitment:* Wanting to be a lifelong learner is the prerequisite for embracing and studying new experiences and ideas and then applying them to your curriculum.

3. *A Recursive Process:* Just as Donald Murray explains in *Write to Learn* (1984), professional study, like the writing process, does not follow a sequence of prescribed steps that's the same for all learners. The process, with elements working together, is recursive, much like a pendulum that slowly sweeps backward before moving forward.

4. *Collaboration:* A necessity for *all* members of the democratic school community, collaboration means administrators, teachers, students, parents, and support staff work in pairs and small groups to study, problem solve, make curricular decisions, and implement teaching interventions that support children's learning.

5. *Cooperation:* Teachers and administrators help one another by sharing materials and resources, modeling minilessons, covering someone's class in an emergency, and accepting and valuing the diversity of expertise among staff members.

6. *Inquiry:* Posing questions quickly reveals the diverse learning needs among administrators and faculty. Inquiry invites the exploration of professional study frameworks that tap into this diversity.

7. *Risk taking:* Principals who are risk takers are comfortable with change and view making mistakes as a key part of the learning process. They construct safe environments where teachers can risk trying new ideas and celebrate errors as an opportunity for continued learning.

8. *Time:* Administrators who applaud professional study find and create time within the school's schedule for teachers to confer and learn.

9. *Reflection and Evaluation:* Learners remember and make connections to experiences, professional articles, and books when there's time to contemplate, talk, and visualize ideas. Self-evaluation, an important aspect of reflection, leads teachers and administrators to a deeper understanding of how they and others learn and fosters the setting of reasonable, doable goals.

10. *Feedback:* Exchanges with more knowledgeable and experienced teachers through coaching and support networks enable teachers to process and clarify new ideas.

Closing Thoughts

To move forward, it's helpful to look backward, for by looking backward, a school community gains insights into its history, comes to know how certain events shaped its climate and environment, and can use these understandings to plan for professional study. The process can highlight differences among teachers and between teachers and administrators. However, if administrators commit to creating an environment that values inquiry and talk, a community can discover its strengths, and through collaborative study, develop congruent beliefs about how children learn and progress.

4
Peer Partners
Surviving the First Year

My first teaching assignment was in a small country school in Gainesboro, Virginia. In August 1963, a month after my husband and I decided to move from New York City to Winchester, Virginia, the Frederick County School Board hired me to teach sixth grade. That year I worked alone in a self-contained classroom. No support from other teachers, no guidance. The children, like the rotating beacon on a lighthouse, led the way as I struggled through a fog, trying to figure out how to teach reading, writing, science, mathematics, and social studies.

Daily mistakes compounded like interest on a bank account, and the voices of the principal and librarian echoed in my mind: "Your students are too noisy when they walk to lunch, Mrs. Robb" or "Children don't walk to the library in single file, they walk with a partner. Single file is for bathroom breaks." By making mistake after mistake, I learned the school's routines for report cards and attendance reports, procedures for recess, and our place in the auditorium during assemblies.

The other teachers were veterans. Routines I found confusing, they completed with little thought. Voices inside my head hounded me: *Why didn't I know this information?* As my anxiety increased, so did my silence. Surely, I would appear inept if I requested help.

All year, only one person watched me teach; the county's director of instruction observed one science lesson in mid-February. Before he left, he said, "Nice lesson," and that was all the feedback I received that year. *But I want more!*, my inner voice shouted.

Helping a first-year teacher who had been tossed into an unfamiliar culture and had no prior teaching experience was not part of the school's agenda.

50

Doubting voices bombarded my waking and sleeping hours. Was I doing a good job? Were students learning enough? How should I group them? What could I do with the rest of the class if I supported students who struggled with reading? Was the basal and workbook the only way to teach reading?

A tight schedule offered no time to chat with other teachers. Everywhere my thirty-three students went, I accompanied them, except when I didn't have lunch or recess duty. Occasionally, when a teacher asked, "How are things going?" my response was a terse but untrue "Fine." I longed to talk about my students, what they could and couldn't do. I longed to observe other teachers to see how they handled students who chatted during lessons or didn't complete their work. I longed for someone to extend an invitation to work together, just as Robert Frost (1975) does in his poem "The Pasture."

> I'm going out to clean the pasture spring;
> I'll only stop to rake the leaves away
> (And wait to watch the water clear, I may):
> I shan't be gone long.—You come too.
>
> I'm going out to fetch the little calf
> That's standing by the mother. It's so young
> It totters when she licks it with her tongue.
> I shan't be gone long.—You come too.

"You come too." Those magical words held for me the promise of a partnership. And like the person in the pasture, I fantasized that I'd learn about teaching by watching and listening and exchanging experiences with colleagues. I longed to enter the "shared world" Gordon Wells writes about in *The Meaning Makers*, "which is continually broadened and enriched by the exchange of stories with others" (1986, 196).

Things haven't radically changed in the almost forty years that have passed. Even today, too many experienced and new teachers work alone. And isolation breeds loneliness and insecurity and can diminish teachers' growth. We need to communicate in order to understand our world. For teachers, their world is the classroom, the school, and the surrounding community.

Mediating and Negotiating Learning

When learners try to make sense out of experiences, they connect prior knowledge and past experiences to what is new. So if a school requires a teacher to implement guided-reading, and that teacher knows nothing about the purposes of guided reading, how to lead guided-reading groups, and taking running records, the task seems as daunting as those Rumplestilt-skin demanded of the miller's daughter.

One way to build knowledge is through conversations with and obser-vations of teachers who have lived through similar situations and problems. Through conversations, the novice can question, listen, and comment, all the time cueing in to the ways other teachers tackle similar problems. Observing how others lead guided-reading groups is a teacher-to-teacher minilesson that provides a model the observer can reflect upon and question. Garth Boomer, in "Negotiating the Curriculum" (1992), invites teachers to be the mediators and negotiators of learning with their students, and I believe that teachers must also become the mediators and negotiators of learning with one another.

The meaningful dialogue that emerges from teachers posing ques-tions can create schools with these knowledge-building partnerships: student-to-student, teacher-to-student, teacher-to-teacher, teacher-to-administrator, parent-to-teacher, and parent-to-student. A school culture that encourages learning partnerships among teachers and administrators nurtures and sup-ports first-year teachers. Such a knowledge-building culture also enables experienced teachers to trade in classroom practices that are familiar and comfortable for practices that improve children's achievement.

Even today, I can readily conjure up the lonely and insecure feelings that dominated my first two years of teaching. Too many teachers with excellent potential leave the profession because they feel isolated and abandoned and experience more frustration than success.

Challenges Facing First-Year Teachers

Thirty to thirty-five new students and a new curriculum, weekly lesson plans, and creating yearlong goals consume most of teachers' time in and out of school. For first-year teachers, these tasks often dominate their waking and sleeping hours. "I can't sleep when it's report card time," a new fourth-grade teacher told me. "It's like I've drunk six cups of coffee—my eyes are wide open. So I plan what I will write in a few narratives about each child, then I close my eyes hoping to sleep. If I'm overly restless, I just get up and jot down notes for my report cards instead of torturing myself by trying to fall asleep."

A first-year reading-writing teacher on the seventh-grade team at a middle school told me, "I dream about what I'm going to teach the next day, and all of the paperwork I can't seem to turn in on time. It's the little things like where and when to send the daily attendance records or learning fire drill procedures that disturbed my equilibrium during my first year of teaching."

Even today, with more than thirty years of teaching experiences, I worry and fret and often feel a thirty-hour day would be ideal. To explore ways to support struggling students, complete report cards at a more reflective pace, or prepare more thoroughly for parent-student-teacher conferences takes time.

An overload of tasks and things to think about affects memory. Throughout my first year of teaching, I joked around with my husband, telling him that I was already suffering the short-term memory loss characteristic of the elderly. But as we talked through my concerns, I recognized that not knowing about school procedures and receiving deadline dates for paperwork a day before the due date imprisoned me in a constant state of worry. Moreover, teaching my students captivated me far more than keeping up with the school's routine tasks. Often, without hesitating, I'd let my overloaded mind put aside these additional duties.

Frequent meetings with a peer partner would have prevented my anxiety and frustrations from rapidly escalating, for a peer could guide me, suggesting ways to budget time so that I completed administrative tasks instead of shoving them aside. Experiences such as these have shaped my thinking about how peer partnerships can support beginning teachers and experienced teachers new to a school.

The Importance of Peer Partnerships

A peer partner is an experienced, nurturing teacher with strong communication and teaching skills who has earned the respect of colleagues. Even though peer partners carry a full teaching load and often do not receive additional salary, they experience great satisfaction from dedicating some time to support beginning teachers and those new to a school. It's helpful, as Mary Delgado (1999) suggests, for administrators to schedule one shared preparation period between the more experienced peer mentor and his or her partner so that there is time for productive conversations about management strategies, classroom events, and students with problems. The suggestions that follow can help you identify worthy candidates for peer partnerships.

- Invite experienced teachers to volunteer for this position. It's crucial for teachers to choose this responsibility. Remember that an invitation allows a teacher to decline without feeling that there will be negative reactions.
- Look for these characteristics in a candidate: good listening skills; flexibility; a positive, upbeat outlook; excellent time-management skills;

willingness to offer students choices; ability to set reasonable goals for self.

- Pair each peer partner with only one new teacher.
- Form a support group for the experienced peers so they can trouble-shoot with one another and brainstorm ways to address issues that arise.
- Meet with volunteers, an administrator, and an experienced peer partner before school officially starts to discuss their responsibilities and create an outline of key events and routines in their school.

Responsibilities of a Peer Partner

Prior to and throughout the school year, a peer partner meets with a new colleague. Meetings can be five-minute on-the-run chats or longer, negotiated conferences. The purpose of these encounters is to familiarize first-year teachers and experienced teachers new to a district with a school's routines and required record keeping. Coping with the routine tasks builds teachers' confidence, bonds them to a colleague, opens meaningful dialogue, and enables them to focus on their teaching.

The following are suggestions for being an effective peer partner.

- View the orientation to a school's culture as an *ongoing process*. It takes time for teachers to understand and independently act upon specific expectations.
- Dispense information close to the time teachers need it because using new data enables teachers to remember it.
- Review discipline, attendance, report, and field trip policies and fire drill procedures several times during the year.
- Listen to a new teacher's concerns and questions to determine areas that need support.
- Maintain a confidential relationship.
- Inform a teacher when interim grades and report cards are due, where to find the forms, and who receives them.
- Prepare teachers for telephone and in-school parent conferences.
- Share ways you handle similar tasks, such as planning and establishing goals, grouping students, classroom behavior, and coping with disgruntled parents. Sharing provides models and problem-solving strategies for new teachers.

Questions New Teachers Ask Peer Partners

Because peer partners meet regularly throughout the school year, new teachers have many opportunities to pose questions. The content of these questions changes as teachers live through their first year.

In August, a new fourth-grade teacher's wonderings centered around daily management tasks: How detailed do lesson plans have to be? Where do I send the attendance reports? How do I arrange for a sub if I'm sick? Do I walk my class to music and physical education? Do I pick them up?

By the end of the first eight weeks of school, her queries dwelled on curriculum and communicating with parents: Are we required to finish a certain number of science and history units? Do you have a completed, sample report card? What do I do if I can't reach parents and they don't return my telephone calls?

The peer partner permits a new teacher to acclimate herself to the school's environment and expectations while providing the support and positive feedback that nurtures self-esteem.

Warren County Junior High School Peer Partner Program

As soon as Evan Robb knew that he would be the principal of Warren County Junior High School, he placed the creation of a peer-partner program at the top of his "to do" list. "I had to develop a peer-partnership program. The school was new, and more than a dozen teachers I hired were new to Warren County; the first year would be a new experience for the entire community," he told me. "My responsibility is to provide supportive frameworks that enable every teacher to experience success and have a productive year. As soon as I hire a teacher, I am committed to helping her develop."

Evan reread and reflected on notes about peer partners that he collected at a conference for administrators. He called several principals to discuss their programs and gather additional ideas. Finally, he drafted a peer-partner program to share with experienced teachers he hired from the middle and high school. Evan wanted peer partners to have a written checklist to which they could refer. "A list diminished the stress of remembering many details and routines in addition to a peer's own responsibilities," Evan pointed out.

Teachers who accepted Evan's invitation and became peer partners reviewed and edited the list. To relieve a buildup of tension among beginning teachers, he encouraged peer partners to share, throughout the year, fears, mistakes, and funny stories from their first year of teaching. As partners completed each section of the plan, they submitted that section, with dates indicating when the item was discussed, to their department chairs.

This program will be evaluated and revised by participants annually to ensure that it adequately supports what teachers want. View the program that follows as suggestions your school can adapt.

Suggested Activity Time Line of Events for August

BT = Beginning Teacher

Fill in the date for completed items in the blank line next to each task:

_____ Welcome your BT partner with a telephone call, introducing yourself, explaining your role, and providing information about the community and school culture.

_____ Schedule a tour of the school building, highlighting important places: mailboxes, classrooms, faculty room, nurses and guidance offices, location of media equipment, teachers parking lot.

_____ Introduce important personnel: secretaries; department heads; guidance counselors; librarians; and music, p.e., art, special ed, and reading teachers.

_____ Provide the following assistance with school procedures:

- Secure and review curriculum guides and textbooks.
- Review the process for completing and turning in beginning-of-school paperwork.
- Review the items in the teacher handbook: fire drill, plan books, sign-in and sign-out sheets, ID badges, leave policy.
- Discuss all schedules that affect the BT.
- Discuss attendance procedures.

_____ Discuss required classroom rules and management systems.

_____ Help the BT arrange classroom and plan for the first day and week.

_____ Share management strategies that work for you: how to set up grade book; keeping track of homework and tardies; organizing the first day and week; using administrators to help.

Suggested Activity Time Line of Events for September

BT = Beginning Teacher

Fill in the date for completed items in the blank line next to each task:

_____ Negotiate meeting and interaction times with BT.

_____ Share your plan book and ask BT if she or he has questions.

_____ Check on how BT is doing with grading and assessment.

_____ Show BT how to set up student work files.

_____ Help BT prioritize workload.

_____ Plan and assist with Back to School Night.

_____ Share ideas of how to successfully interact with parents.

_____ Model for BT positive-feedback telephone calls to parents.

_____ Review leave procedures and engaging a substitute.

_____ Review field trip policies and procedures.

_____ Discuss professional study opportunities.

_____ Discuss religious holiday policies.

_____ Show location and use of students' cumulative folders and health files.

Suggested Activity Time Line of Events for October–December

BT = Beginning Teacher

Fill in the date for completed items in the blank line next to each task:

_____ Provide assistance for the BT during the first interim and grading period: comments, grading system, computerized grading.

_____ Review snow-day policies and schedule changes.

_____ Assist BT in planning first parent conferences.

_____ Review grading system and any special forms to be completed.

_____ Review referral process for child study and special education.

_____ Encourage BT to observe other teachers, including yourself. Ask administrators to cover BT's class.

_____ Celebrate positives BT shares; be sympathetic to BT's concerns. If necessary, negotiate with BT, asking for administrative support.

_____ Visit BT's classroom as a supporter, not an evaluator.

Suggested Activity Time Line of Events for January–February

BT = Beginning Teacher

Fill in the date for completed items in the blank line next to each task:

_____ Review policies and issues regarding retention and failure of students.

_____ Discuss exam policies and share old exams with BT.

_____ Review end-of-semester grading policies and procedures.

_____ Review curriculum guides and discuss upcoming topics.

_____ Prepare BT for midyear conference with principal.

Suggested Activity Time Line of Events for March–June

BT = Beginning Teacher

Fill in the date for completed items in the blank line next to each task:

_____ Share suggestions for maintaining students' interest at the end of the year.

_____ Share how you reduce end-of-the-year stress levels.

_____ Review these policies:

- updating literacy profiles and cumulative folders
- completing retention procedures if necessary
- completing final grade reports
- following "closing the year" procedures

_____ Take the time to celebrate all the first-year successes!

Closing Thoughts

Every school can easily begin professional study by creating a peer-partner program. It costs no extra money, it taps into the strengths of experienced teachers, and it reduces the stress teachers experience as they adjust to a new profession and/or school. Here are some questions for school administrators to consider as they develop a peer-partner program:

- What kind of training should the school offer?
- Can I find time during the school day for peer-partner support-group meetings?
- Should we develop a time line of events and routines?
- Who will evaluate and revise the program?
- Am I periodically writing celebratory and appreciative notes to peer partners and new teachers?

5

Coaches and Lead Teachers

Collaborating with an expert, such as a coach or lead teacher, is a satisfying way to learn because together you build, clarify, and refine new and innovative teaching practices. Halfway through the first year I coached Kathleen Hobbs, a young, talented reading-writing teacher at my school. She explained her feelings about team teaching during one of our follow-up meetings: "I loved our sideline chat after we made the rounds and watched students adjust their predictions. We both noticed the boy revising without returning to his book to confirm his adjustments. Alone, I would have confronted him and probably increased my frustration. But after our minimeeting, I placed a copy on his desk and gently asked him to use the book. At that point I realized that I'd accomplish more by talking to him after class to discover why he didn't have a book than addressing the problem publicly." Coaching Kathleen and teaching with her provided countless opportunities for both of us to grow through conversations about children, books, managing a reading-writing workshop, and teaching strategies—and that's the purpose of the coaching relationship.

The Art of Coaching Teachers

Master teachers who have taught many grade levels, teacher trainers who work at universities and conduct research in classrooms, and consultants who have years of classroom experience can all effectively coach teachers. In my opinion, coaches who continue to teach their own students can better understand how the daily scheduling, management, and student behavior issues affect teaching because they grapple with them, too. In addition to having teaching expertise, it's crucial for a coach to be able to accept a teacher where she or he is, find common talking points to build a trusting relationship, then help the teacher travel to other places.

A coach is a lifelong learner who can design, develop, implement, and monitor curriculum. From classroom experience, a coach has developed instructional strategies that reflect current best practices and research. Skilled in classroom management, the coach can also assess and evaluate students in order to flexibly group them and meet each child's needs.

I call coaching an art, for coaching involves the fine art of interacting with another professional. The goal of all coaches, whether they work with a tennis player, opera singer, or teacher, is to improve that person's performance. However, the purpose of coaching teachers moves beyond creating an individual star to improving the learning of children.

The coach listens, nurtures, provides feedback, and senses when to maintain the status quo and when to pose questions that gently nudge a teacher forward without harming self-esteem and confidence. Just like an artist, the teacher chooses the subject to be explored, and instead of painting, he or she uses words to express his or her feelings with a colleague. "I waited until you worked with two of my friends before I invited you into my classroom," a teacher at Keister Elementary told me. "I wanted to know what you were *really* like before I took a chance." Accepting an invitation from a coach is "taking a chance" on a relationship with someone you might not know well. It's a courageous step into uncharted territory.

The coach supports the teacher's explorations of a subject by listening, observing, posing questions, conversing, and suggesting books and journal articles that can enlarge and extend the teacher's knowledge. The primary goal is to build on what a teacher knows and does well. As a trusting relationship develops, the coach often models a strategy and team teaches.

Two questions guide my coaching: (1) What do you think worked well? (2) Do you have any questions about anything that happened during the lesson or where you might go? These questions focus the teacher on his or her practices and students' learning.

At Johnson Williams Middle School in Berryville, Virginia, sixth-grade teacher Peggy Wampler responded to my questions by discussing her minilesson and follow-up class on writing leads. "I do a good job modeling how I open a piece with a question or an unusual fact," Peggy told me, "and my students can revise their leads using one of those techniques. But I always avoid showing how I can grab the reader with dialogue or a short anecdote. I'm uncomfortable with those."

"Let me also point out what I thought worked so well," I replied. "Students were glued to the chart as you presented the lesson. I was impressed with their thoughtful questions and noticed that during workshop, several wrote two alternate leads. Would you like to work on other kinds of leads?" I asked. "Or did you have something else in mind?" My goal was for Peggy to lead the way; I would follow with support and suggestions.

"I want to show students other ways to start a piece," Peggy said. So together, we planned a lesson that invited students to read and analyze the leads in their free-choice library books. Meanwhile, I asked Peggy to find several books that open with dialogue or an anecdote, and I promised to bring some of my favorite titles to our next meeting.

My first question emphasized what worked and focused Peggy on the effects her teaching had on her sixth graders. It also gave me the opportunity to expand Peggy's positive feedback and point to specific student behaviors. The second question invites the teacher to assess his or her needs and choose what we will work on together. My goal is to teach teachers how to reflect on a lesson and use their reflections to celebrate what worked, then identify an area that requires more thought, dialogue, and research. "These two questions," I tell Peggy, "steer my teaching." I want Peggy to know that even after years of experience, I still self-evaluate. I've come to know that taking risks, making mistakes, and reflecting on the experience are ideal ways to progress as a teacher.

Selecting a Coach

Though coaching styles differ, a coach must have a great deal of knowledge about teaching, keep abreast of research by reading professional journals and books, and have direct teaching experience in different grades. The following is a list of ten qualities the teachers at Keister Elementary School put together as they searched for a visiting coach-consultant. A coach should:

- have a passion for teaching children
- have a minimum of fifteen years of teaching experience in different grades
- currently be teaching children
- be nurturing, supportive, and an active listener
- have experience in teaching teachers
- share teaching ideas and personal experiences

- listen and be nonjudgmental
- respect teachers' needs
- feel comfortable modeling and team teaching at all elementary school grades
- provide teachers with professional resources

Coaches can be members of a school's faculty, master teachers from the school district, or outside consultants. Freeing a classroom teacher to coach others in a school might seem like a problem. However, by hiring a substitute teacher for three to four blocks of time each month or by reducing a teacher's schedule and hiring another teacher, the problem is solved. Classroom teachers who coach bring back innovative ideas to their schools that can benefit children, teachers, and parents.

Trust: The Backbone of a Teacher-Coach Relationship

For a productive relationship to develop between coach and teacher, both must come to trust one another. That's why a coach cannot be an evaluator or a person who reports mistakes and inadequacies to an administrator. I'm up-front with a principal, and before I accept a coaching position, I present my standard speech. "This is a confidential relationship," I explain. "Teachers who take risks will make mistakes—I hope they make mistakes, for that's how learners grow. I'm not going to file reports on each coaching session. However, I will encourage the teacher to share what's happening in the classroom with you. At some point, she'll probably invite you into her room and involve you with the children."

A coach is not a double agent working for administrators and teachers. A principal hires a coach—someone he or she trusts enough to effect change—then allows the coach to develop meaningful, confidential relationships with teachers. Without confidentiality, trust rarely develops.

Each time I extend an invitation to a teacher, the words of my then-teenage daughter, Anina, ring in my head: *When will you learn, Mom, that every time you tell me what to do, I want to do the opposite?* The lesson I learned from Anina—to offer choices—is one I apply to my coaching. Implied in the invitation is the respect for teachers' right to decide whether they want to work with me. Choice, then, is the prerequisite for change.

Whether I'm coaching teachers at my school, at a school close to home where teachers and I know one another, or in schools far from home, I always extend invitations. For with invitations, meaningful collaborations can develop.

Coaching on Home Turf

My schedule at Powhatan is compressed into three days, leaving me time to write and work in public schools. In addition to teaching double periods of reading-writing workshop to eighth graders, I coach teachers, organize parent and teacher study groups, and lead monthly staff development workshops.

Annually, I negotiate my coaching schedule with John Lathrop, Powhatan's head. Invitations from experienced teachers and goals that faculty and I have established at professional study workshops affect these negotiations. Rethinking and redefining my job each year enables me to respond to teachers' questions and needs.

The school requires that I coach new, inexperienced teachers, and makes this clear to new teachers before they sign a contract. It's crucial to be up-front with such a requirement. Forcing even a novice teacher into a coaching relationship can be unproductive.

New teachers and I meet once a week throughout the year, and teachers can request additional time when they need it. These meetings open with a list of questions that the teacher has jotted down. I encourage teachers to keep a running record of their questions, emphasizing that every query is important. A new fifth-grade teacher asks me to help him administer spelling inventories, a fourth-grade teacher wonders how she can manage four different book discussion groups, and a kindergarten teacher wants to try interactive writing with her students. Some teachers work through a teaching strategy with me, then try it while I watch. Others ask me to model while they observe and note questions to discuss later that day.

I meet with a new teacher two weeks before school opens. He will teach reading-writing workshop to sixth and seventh graders. His goal is to "survive the first day," and together, we discuss ideas and make plans. After a new teacher successfully completes the first day and week, anxiety levels slowly diminish, and coaching meetings can turn to raising and discussing questions regarding teaching strategies, grouping students, record keeping, and assessment and evaluation.

Coaching at my school differs in many ways from coaching one day a month in another district. I stay in closer touch with teachers I'm coaching on my home turf because of the following reasons:

- I can interact with teachers frequently, respond to their questions quickly, and observe them many times.
- I can follow up if a project develops kinks and negotiate additional meetings and observations for those teachers.

- I can work through an issue over several days by being a good listener and posing questions that enable the teacher to express salient issues and needs.

- I can carve out the time to work with a teacher who extends an invitation after my fall schedule has been planned. I always expect additional invitations, for it is impossible to predict needs for half a year.

- I can troubleshoot before negative feelings escalate when a teacher feels apprehensive about how a strategy is working in her class. Immediate, face-to-face discussions are more effective than e-mail and telephone conversations because I can read and respond to body language and facial expressions.

- I can immediately celebrate progress and success.

- I can provide materials and resources quickly.

- I can make impromptu visits to classrooms to observe how a teacher is managing, especially if I'm receiving little feedback from that teacher.

Coaching Stories from My School

In mid-October, Debi Gustin, who's been teaching first grade at Powhatan for six years, invites me into her classroom. "I need help with research and writing," she says. In order to spend two one-hour sessions in Debi's class and meet with her for thirty minutes each week, I juggle my schedule, taking time from teachers who agree to give up one of my visits for several weeks.

We schedule a meeting time on Monday, and Debi asks me how she can help first graders research farm animals without copying words from books. "Tell me what you've been doing," I say.

"I let them look through books, study pictures, and read simple texts for one period. They have to find three facts and write three sentences about their animal. Children take notes, but they always copy words out of the book."

"How much time do you think you might need to learn new information?" I ask.

"Oh, a lot of time—until I could think about the topic without looking in the books. I guess I need to do the same for my students."

I build on Debi's realization and suggest that she allow the children to browse through and study books over three to four days. "Each day," I suggest, "stop ten minutes before the class ends and invite the children to share one thing they learned." Then I model a double-entry note-taking process for Debi to demonstrate to her children. On the left side of the paper, ask the chil-

The Baby Swans are called cienits.

Swans Travel sorth Like any other Brids in the winter

Swans pek ther fethers, lik sea Gulls, so they get the oil on ther bills, then they rub it on ther fethers, so ther fether dant eet wet,

Figure 5–1. Eliza's picture

dren to draw, from memory, each fact learned. On the right side, have them use words to tell about each picture. This will be their plan for writing. But before inviting them to write, Debi and I model by thinking aloud and writing on chart paper how to decide which fact to start with and how we go about drafting the piece.

Though it takes Debi's first graders four one-hour sessions to read and two one-hour sessions to plan before they write, she tells me, "The time I allowed the children to read, think, and talk, along with your modeling and our answering their questions made such a difference." Debi and I grin and nod to one another as we watch Finn write about his drawings. It's mid-October and for the first time Finn doesn't ask Debi to write for him. He explains it this way: "My pictures did the thinking so the writing was easier."

Eliza takes time to draw her facts in great detail before writing her notes (see Figure 5–1). Her draft shows how she internalized our modeling and elaborated on her notes. She opens her piece with a question, just as I did when I wrote about hippopotami (see Figures 5–2 and 5–3). Note how Eliza moves beyond her three facts, something Debi and I encouraged the children to do.

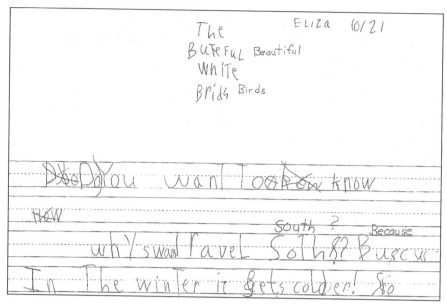

Figure 5–2. Eliza's written draft

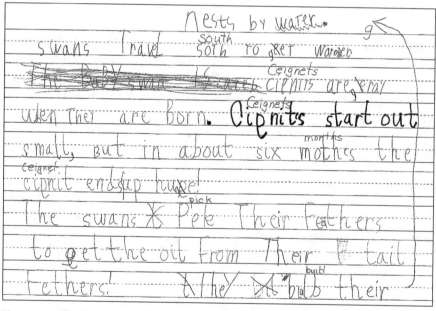

Figure 5–3. Eliza's written draft

Each day before workshop starts, Debi asks the children to tell her what they remember about writing a report. On the day Debi and I introduce and model writing a final draft, here's what students tell us:

1. We picked an animal.
2. We read lots and talked to a partner after each reading.
3. We did a double-sided brainstorm: pictures of three facts and we wrote about the pictures.
4. We started the writing with a favorite fact.
5. We added other facts. We added more.
6. We read our work to Mrs. Gustin or Mrs. Robb. They helped us with spelling and punctuation.

While reviewing the process we encouraged students to pose questions; we wanted many opportunities to clarify their understandings. Daily recaps of the process by students along with minilessons deepened students' knowledge of research because it raised their awareness of complex strategies.

How Coaching Effects Change: One Teacher's Story

Anne Wheeler, Powhatan's librarian, was a peer evaluator for sixth-grade history teacher Dick Bell, who has taught at Powhatan for more than twenty years. In the spring, Dick invited Anne to evaluate him the following year. They negotiated goals that Anne would support throughout the year.

Based on the results of informal reading inventories and standardized testing, Dick's class of twenty-four students had a range of reading abilities from third to eighth grade. Anne and Dick requested a meeting with me after Dick had introduced the required research project and presented students with a sheet of guidelines. Written with behavioral goals, each of the six requirements opened with "You will." Students had to choose a topic, use two trade books, take notes on index cards, create a writing plan or outline, include a bibliography, and write a report that was from one and a half to three double-spaced typed pages. Due dates for each step were on the chalkboard for students to record on their sheets.

Though I felt overwhelmed with the list of "You wills" and all of the deadline dates, I said nothing. My goal was for Dick to come to this realization on his own. And so I adopted the role of listener, inviting him to talk.

"Tell me about your research project and students' reactions," I said.

"I struggled all year with the required sixth-grade research project," Dick answered. "I avoided starting because I knew it was too difficult for lots of my students. But when the second week in April arrived, time was running out, so I handed them my research guideline sheet."

Then Dick asked me to help him with students who were having a tough time choosing a topic and finding books. Both Anne and Dick verbalized issues that frustrated students:

Choosing and narrowing a topic   One student insisted she could write a three-page report on Japanese gardens; another wanted to write about all of Leonardo DaVinci's inventions.

Concentrating while reading   Many students socialized during this time. "Why can't I do the work at home?" was a typical question.

Wanting to use the Internet as the only source   Many demanded, "Why can't we just take stuff off the Internet? It's all in one place."

Taking notes   "How do I do it?" "Why on index cards?" "How do I know what's important?" were common queries.

Knowing how to make a plan   Student comments included "I can't outline." "How many paragraphs?" "I can't do this in school." "We should do it all at home." (In order to learn, Dick wanted his students to go through a process at school—even if this meant struggling with taking notes, planning, and drafting.)

At first, finding the time to support Dick and Anne during the last trimester seemed impossible. My schedule was full. So I met with teachers I was coaching, explained the situation, and invited them to help me discover possible solutions. Two teachers volunteered to relinquish one period so I could work with Dick while he taught sixth-grade history.

It's easier to unilaterally make such decisions, but it's a strategy coaches must resist. If coaching is a partnership based on mutual trust and respect, the teachers in a coaching relationship should be an important part of any decisions that affect them.

After Anne and Dick reviewed students' feelings toward research with me, I suggested that we gather more data by posing these questions to them: What are your attitudes toward research? Why do people do research? What are the steps/processes we use to research a topic? What things do we need help with?

We organized students into groups of four and five. Over two days, they discussed these questions, and I recorded their responses on chart paper. There was not one positive comment; thirty-one negative comments described students' attitude toward research and Dick's guideline sheet: *Date is too limiting. It's boring. Hard to find books we can read. Not enough time. Not good at it.* "Well," Dick said, "given my doubts over students' readiness for this project, their remarks don't surprise me."

Because Dick had many years of teaching experience, he was able to deal with students' comments, yet I didn't want discouraged feelings to escalate. "You know," I said, "this is a great opportunity to develop strategies for students who have little knowledge of the research process. Besides," I added, "the fact that students were honest says a great deal about their relationship with you. They feel comfortable telling you why the project is too difficult, knowing that you'll explore ways to support them."

Students' candid comments showed us how little they knew about the process of researching a topic: *find information, make an outline, turn in a final draft* summarized their knowledge. Under "Things They Need Help On," students listed important strategies such as *getting feedback about your topic, using a table of contents and index to locate information, managing time, sorting—knowing which information you did or did not need, keeping track of information.* Only one purpose for research echoed through the classroom: *It's what teachers make you do.*

Dick, Anne, and I met and pored over students' feedback. I cheered Dick by pointing out that the students had provided the framework for his teaching. Each day, Dick presented minilessons that grew out of students' comments. He also identified many additional minilesson topics as students lived through the researching experience.

Now Anne, Dick, and I worked to relieve students' frustration with not finding enough material, keeping track of materials, changing a topic midstream, and negotiating more reasonable deadline dates. Dick paled when I said, "I don't care if they never write a draft; if they learn everything up to that point, then the writing will be easy."

At a later meeting, Dick told me and Anne, "I quaked when Laura said that—it shattered everything I believed about research papers." Once Dick tossed out his hidden agenda, pressure diminished. To his surprise, every student completed a paper, though at different times. We also discovered that with such a large class, having three teachers available to support students was crucial to the project's success.

To guide students through the complex research process, Dick created a research checklist that posed questions such as:

- Have you been writing daily about your reading?
- Have you gathered your required sources?
- Have you broken your subjects into five parts—three that explain your topic to your audience and two that interest you?
- Have you written three specific note cards from your reading about each aspect?
- Have you had your first draft peer edited?
- Has the teacher read your first draft?

However, the long list of twenty things to do raised the anxiety levels of many students. "Next year," Dick said, "I'll divide the list into five separate sections: reading, focusing, taking notes, planning, and drafting."

During the last week of school, Dick posed the same four questions asked at the start of the project. Students' responses illustrated their improved attitudes toward and knowledge of the research process. Instead of thirty-one negative comments under "Our Attitude Toward Research," students made ten positive comments. One shot to the core of student research: *Research is great and enjoyable when the topic interests you.* Only one student said *Boring, tedious, annoying.*

Experiencing and then reflecting on researching deepened students' knowledge of the process, and their comments illustrated this heightened awareness: *Look in an encyclopedia for a topic overview and a list of resources. Read, close the book, then take notes.* The Readers Guide to Periodicals *is a great resource. Write what you remember. Reread parts until you can think about them in your head without reading.*

It's important to point out their list of "Things We Need Help On" was similar to the first list. Anne, Dick, and I felt students recognized that this research experience was a beginning; they understood that teacher modeling and support would be necessary in subsequent years. Instead of a smug "We know it all," students expressed their respect for a complex process by explaining that next year research might be easier, but they'd still have similar questions.

Even though Anne, Dick, and I hoped that students would now see research in a broader context and realize that breakthroughs in medicine, immunization, manufacturing, and technology resulted from research, this didn't happen. However, they had moved beyond "It's what teachers make you do," to "You can learn so much, and it can help if you're writing a story." The three adults put their disappointment aside and agreed that students had made meaningful research connections and deepened their knowledge of the process. Fulfilling our agenda was an unfair expectation.

Coaching Beyond Home Turf

One Tuesday a month, I spend the day coaching teachers at Keister Elementary School in Harrisonburg, Virginia. Since I cannot support teachers during the weeks between each visit, I offer teachers feedback and clarification on the telephone or by e-mail. This arrangement places the responsibility for daily support on the principal, her assistant, and experienced teachers. When teachers try a new strategy, many require that someone visit their classroom and confer with them about the effectiveness of modeling and monitoring the strategy, as well as suggesting classroom-management tips. Therefore, the success of long-distance coaching depends upon the instructional leadership and commitment of the principal and other school administrators who provide the scaffolding teachers require.

One week prior to my visit, Ann Conners, the principal, faxes me a schedule and letters from teachers. Between 10:00 A.M. and 3:00 P.M. I visit three to five classes.

In their letters, teachers describe what I will be observing, or they invite me to model a reading or writing strategy. They also pose questions that we will discuss during our one-on-one conferences. Questions, like the sampling that follows, cover a wide range of topics.

- Am I visiting enough students during writing workshop?
- How can I include the predict/support strategy in students' free-choice reading?
- What types of authentic reading activities can students not participating in guided reading do?
- How can I show students what a productive literature discussion group looks like?
- What does shared writing look like in a first-grade classroom?

Often, I'll respond to a teacher's question by posing a question. I do this to stir and extend his or her thinking. My hope is that the teacher's thoughts will provide me with ideas for opening a dialogue. To pose questions that stimulate reflection means I have to be a careful and thoughtful listener. Even more important, questions are kinder and show the respect I have for a teacher. A didactic response that implies "My way is the only way" raises hackles and increases anger. Questions, on the other hand, are gentle and offer choices, not criticism.

Third-grade teacher Debbie Rodefer asked me, "Do I have to make up questions for students to answer after every chapter of our first book, *Sarah, Plain and Tall?*"

"What would you like to do if you were reading *Sarah, Plain and Tall?*" I asked. Silence.

The reply came several minutes later. "I don't think I'd stop after each chapter, and I'm not sure I'd want to keep answering questions."

"You might want to divide the book into three chunks and invite students to create discussion questions after each section," I suggested.

"But what if their questions are all factual?"

"Could you teach them how to pose open-ended questions?" I asked. And Debbie nodded.

Next time I visited, Debbie shared discussion questions that groups of third graders composed for the first three chapters. Elated about what her students had accomplished, Debbie told me: "Aren't these questions terrific? They love discussing them. And I have more time to focus on watching children and thinking about their work."

Third Graders' Questions for *Sarah, Plain and Tall*

Each group chose one of their questions to share. If groups duplicated a question, then they had others to contribute.

1. Why does Anna want Papa to find out if Sarah sings?
2. Why do Anna and Caleb worry about Sarah staying?
3. Why does Papa ask the children if Sarah should come?
4. Why do the children think Sarah won't stay?

To compose quality discussion questions, readers reread and think about the text. My goal is to turn as much of the learning over to students, so I have time to watch them at work. What teachers notice about their students can improve teaching practices and children's learning.

In her letter to me, fourth-grade teacher Sandy Palmer wrote: "I do lots of predicting and supporting with whole and small groups, recording students' ideas on chart paper. How can I bring the predict and support strategy to students' free choice reading books?"

We discussed helping students place sticky notes on the front cover of a picture book, halfway through, and two pages before the end. At the top of the sticky note, students place their name and the date, then pause to predict and offer support. Small groups can discuss their books by sharing predictions. I suggested that Sandy keep these in students' reading folders so she could monitor progress, and Sandy took off with this strategy, starting in October and continuing through June.

With short chapter books, Sandy placed sticky notes on the cover, after the second chapter, and two chapters from the end. "My students love this strategy," she tells me. "They have lots to discuss in groups or with a partner, it introduces my kids to new titles, I can track their progress, and they learn to follow directions because they place the sticky notes in books. It's the content I focus on, not the punctuation. Students write quickly because they want to return to the story" (see Figures 5–4a and 5–4b). Sandy's enthusiasm for this strategy rapidly spread to other teachers as she chatted about her student's work.

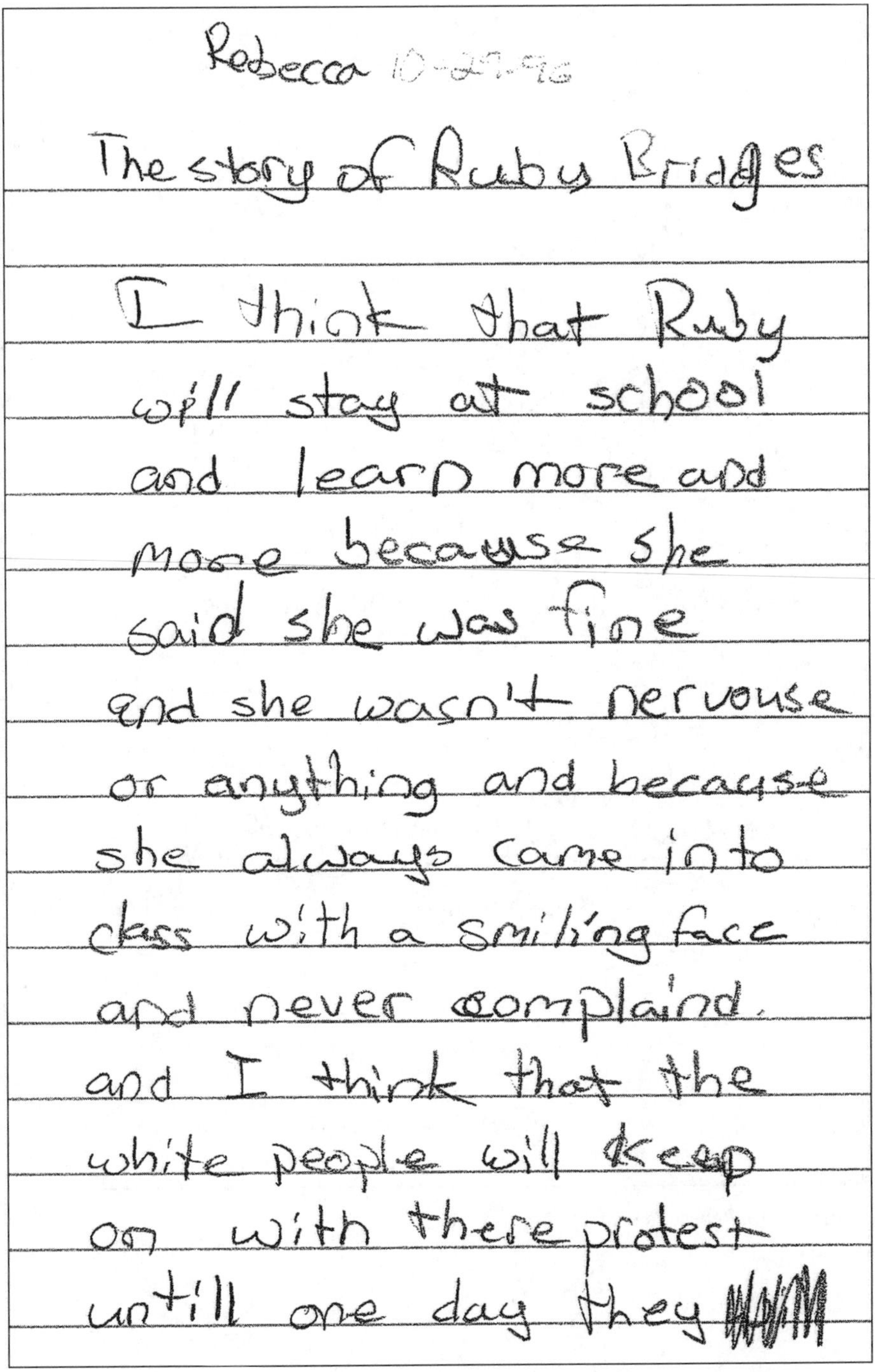

Rebecca 10-29-96

The story of Ruby Bridges

I think that Ruby will stay at school and learn more and more because she said she was fine and she wasn't nervouse or anything and because she always came into class with a smiling face and never complaind. and I think that the white people will keep on with there protest untill one day they

Figure 5–4a. Rebecca's Post-It

will get tierd of
protesting and learn
to like the blak people
and go back to school
and make fraends with
the black people and
they will all go to the
same school.

I was verry right
the way I found that
out was by reading the
afterwards.

Figure 5–4b. Rebecca's Post-It

Some Guidelines for Coaches

- After a teacher accepts an invitation, negotiate with the teacher several long blocks of time to visit his or her classroom. While visiting, circulate, participate, and support the students.

- Schedule time to confer when it's convenient for the teacher. Discover the teacher's goals and mutually set a short-term goal.

- Listen well.

- Plan lessons with a teacher before you observe, model, or team teach.

- Offer choices. Let the teacher decide if he or she wants to practice with you and then teach; have you model the lesson; or team teach. Beforehand, establish the team concept that encourages each person to jump in with questions or suggestions during the lesson.

- Explain that the teacher remains in the room and takes notes if you model a strategy.

- Ask thought-provoking questions. Model for the teacher how posing questions can improve teaching and students' learning.

- Honor a teacher who is willing to change by celebrating growth with a note or a telephone call.

- Accept the teacher where she or he is and gently move her or him forward.

- Build on what a teacher does well. Stress the positive, yet offer suggestions for growth.

- Maintain confidentiality. Build trust through negotiation, choice, shared study, and conversation.

- Point out how students' feedback can improve teaching and invite the teacher to ask students to participate in the evaluative process.

- Help a teacher become reflective and self-evaluative.

- Be a collector. Keep a binder with copies of articles and strategies you want to share. Have a section for each teacher you're coaching that includes observational notes you've made, goals established, teacher queries, and teacher requests that you need to address.

- Encourage a teacher to communicate the changes in her classroom to administrators by sharing student work and by inviting them in to observe.

Coping with Negative Reactions

Each year, our friends who grow organic apples share their bounty with us. In August, George and Bobbi Kessler deliver the first pickings, a basket of red and golden delicious apples. "Cut them open before you bite," they caution. "You might find a worm." We joke about worms being protein, but my husband and I never fail to halve each fruit before delighting in its sweet, juicy flavors. Occasionally, we find a small worm who has taken up residence inside the apple. Carefully, we place apple and worm in our backyard, hoping the creature will peacefully live out its life.

Coaching is similar to halving organically grown apples. Most apples are worm-free, just as most coaching experiences are positive, and the flavor of the relationship grows and lingers. Occasionally, like the wormy apples, a negative experience appears. Only in that case, I can't remove the experience and place it outside. Instead, it's my responsibility to accept and deal with it. Often, coping with a negative coaching relationship is a painful task, as the following anecdote illustrates.

Four angry kindergarten teachers glared at me. They refused to discuss "Theory Becomes Practice at the Point of Interaction" by Linda Fielding and Cathy Roller (1998). Halfway through the section called "Vygotskian Frame," they put the article aside and would not discuss the Zone of Proximal Development. Resistant to the idea that through teacher modeling, think-alouds, and scaffolding, children can learn tasks too difficult to accomplish on their own, they had closed their minds.

In my early teaching days, such a response would have sent my self-esteem plummeting. On that day what rankled me was that these teachers had passed judgment on a theory before exploring and understanding it. Closed minds, like closed doors, often take time to rattle and unlock. My job was to put aside personal frustrations, find common ground, and build enough trust between myself and these teachers so that we could engage in meaningful dialogue. Time, patience, a nonthreatening stance, and inviting them to share teaching strategies enabled relationships to develop. Only then could coaching begin.

One of my toughest coaching assignments was at a middle school. A seventh-grade English teacher invited me into his classroom. However, I did not know that the principal and superintendent had required the invitation.

During meetings, the teacher and I talked about changing round-robin reading and implementing reading workshop so students could read at their independent levels. We discussed writing workshop and minilessons. "I'll think about starting writing workshop," he'd say, but we never moved beyond that point. Discussions were lively and enjoyable, and I believed that in time, he might risk some change.

Weeks later, he told me that he was leaving teaching. "I don't want to change what I've done," he said. "And I never wanted you in my classroom. I *had* to invite you. I won't stop the worksheets and workbooks. I've used them for more than twenty-five years. So you might as well find someone else to help." That was our last meeting.

Downcast and depressed, I mumbled, "I hope things turn out well for you." I had been in a lose-lose situation because teacher improvement had been mandated. Therefore, commitment to growth never developed.

Coaching is like teaching. I want to reach and touch the learning lives of all my students, but that doesn't always happen. The best I can do is reflect on negative experiences, try to learn from each one, and apply these understandings to similar situations.

Lead Teachers

Dr. Glenn Burdick, the superintendent of Winchester Public Schools and Nikki Isherwood, Winchester's director of instruction, integrated the role of coach and peer partner and developed an innovative program that they called Lead Teachers. Both administrators wanted experienced and dedicated teachers to have leadership roles in each of their four elementary schools. If the program worked, lead teachers would be trained for Winchester's middle and high school. Extra budget dollars for these positions came from the salaries of the assistant superintendent and the elementary director of instruction, who had retired. Dr. Burdick believed that students and teachers would benefit if coaches were available in each school to improve instruction and learning.

Lead teachers would leave the classroom for only four to five years; then they would return to the classroom, and a new group would receive training. The administration's goal was to place outstanding, experienced teachers in a coaching and resource role. "This experience," Nikki Isherwood said, "would be growth opportunity for classroom and lead teachers. We believe that respected teachers can reach their peers and effect change. When a lead teachers returns to the classroom, she has grown and enlarged her knowledge about education and continues to benefit students and peers."

In 1996, teachers in Winchester's four elementary schools received the job description for lead teachers, which included the following duties:

1. Meet regularly with principals and the director of instruction to design and develop curriculum in grades K to five.

2. Support new teachers, conferring with them during their first year and introducing them to other faculty.

3. Provide advice on teaching strategies, curriculum, and classroom management to teachers in their schools.

4. Share professional articles, books, and information collected at conferences and classes.

5. Offer to help plan lessons, team teach, and model a strategy in classrooms.

6. Act as a liaison between teachers and the director of instruction.

7. Confer frequently with grade-level team leaders to discuss curriculum and instructional needs.

Unlike a coach, lead teachers are required to report progress to principals and the director of instruction, even though they extend invitations to their faculty.

Training Lead Teachers

Nikki Isherwood asked me to have several training sessions for the lead teachers in August. In addition, she wanted the four lead teachers and me to meet bimonthly through the 1996–1997 school year. During these meetings we'd collaborate to problem solve, and I would model strategies, invite them to practice minilessons before the group, and respond to questions.

Three two-hour sessions in August focused on discussing the role of a coach as well as questions the four teachers collected and raised:

- What happens if a colleague asks us to do something that's not part of our job?
- What if a close friend expects special favors?
- Will they view us as a substitute teacher who gives them a break?
- Will teachers resent us now that we work with them and the administration?

Role playing at each training session relieved some tension. Nikki Isherwood and I asked the questions: Can you cover my class this morning? Will you photocopy these papers for me? Can you make plans for teaching this book? Will you choose two trade books for my class? Will you teach this unit for me?

We practiced and fine-tuned responses that honored the way a teacher felt, such as: "I understand how frustrated (angry, sad, upset) you are. How can I help?" "I hear the concern in your voice, but the only person who can help you is . . ." "I'm delighted to listen, but I can't step in." Anita Jenkins, lead teacher at Virginia Avenue School, told me, "The role plays and suggestions helped me feel I was offering teachers some kind of support, not flatly turning a request down."

To reduce confusion, I asked the lead teachers to explain the guidelines of their new job at opening faculty meetings and review these during the year. In addition, I encouraged them to write notes to teachers that celebrated the good things they observed. "When I'm feeling discouraged or I've had a bad day," a kindergarten teacher tells me, "I reread your note complimenting me on the interactive letter writing you saw." Such notes build self-esteem by spotlighting what worked; they also offer solace at low points in our teaching journeys.

Throughout the year we traded strategies, stories, and presentations. Anita Jenkins told us, "I was shocked when a fifth-grade teacher invited me to help him with the predict/support/confirm/adjust strategies. He was the last person I expected to invite me—he was still into basals and workbooks. He told me that a presentation I made at a fifth-grade team meeting hooked him. Now the entire team wants to work with me."

Ruth Ann Martin discussed how teachers tried to find her but never knew where she was. She gave us copies of weekly schedules that listed where she'd be throughout each day. Once Ruth Ann began posting schedules on her office door, she received a flood of positive feedback. "My teachers appreciated the schedule. I jot down changes," she told us. "If someone felt they needed me immediately, I was easy to find." As we collaborated to help other teachers, we grew professionally by exchanging ideas and titles of trade and professional books and by observing one another.

Closing Thoughts

A coach personalizes teachers' learning by sharing stories and experiences that deepen the bonds of this meaningful relationship. To organize an effective coaching and/or lead teacher program requires credible and respected administrators who can

- recognize the need, remove impediments, and initiate the journey;
- support excellent initiatives whether they originate from teachers, the principal, or the central office; and
- explain passionately and clearly to staff, administrators, parents, local businesses, and the press that a primary goal of having coaches and lead teachers is to construct a common vision.

6

Study Groups
Learning by Doing

A teary, first-year humanities teacher asked to meet with me. She had been given two classes, each with thirty of the weakest students in the seventh grade. One month into the school year she felt defeated, isolated, and ready to quit. She lacked the experience and the background knowledge to assess and support a group of students who refused to read and write and spent the period doodling and chatting. Her decision-making processes repeatedly defaulted because she didn't know how to react to negative comments or how to involve students in learning. At this point, the school did not have a peer-mentoring program.

Monthly meetings with me helped this teacher limp through the year. How to teach and manage this class, however, continued to pose challenges and difficulties because, in one year, it's impossible to gain enough knowledge and experience to meet the needs of struggling readers and writers.

Undergraduate classes had not prepared this novice teacher for coping with students who refused to work and students who could not read the books the district required her to teach. At college, she had planned lessons for an imaginary group of students who always cooperated and worked diligently to meet goals. Both of her student-teaching assignments were in middle-class suburbs with twenty to twenty-four cooperative students. Tossed into a room of young adolescents who had experienced failure for many years, she felt overwhelmed and consumed with thoughts of finding another career.

This story raises three questions:

1. Why are novice instead of experienced teachers working with students who struggle to read and have a history of failure?

2. How does experience and theoretical background knowledge affect teachers' decision-making process?

3. What is an effective way for teachers to continue to learn while they are teaching?

Responses to these questions are important to consider because they have a direct impact on teachers' confidence and continuing professional development. I've based the discussion of the three queries that follow on my teaching, coaching, and consulting experiences.

1. Why are novice instead of experienced teachers working with students who struggle to read and have a history of failure?
   Response: Many schools "reward" experienced teachers by inviting them to teach higher-achieving students or heterogeneous classes with few struggling readers. However, reversing this practice can benefit high-risk students who need the expertise of experienced teachers.

2. How does experience and theoretical background knowledge affect teachers' decision-making process?
   Response: Informed action—the ability to discover ways to make teaching and learning decisions that respond to students' needs— requires that teachers have a theoretical base of knowledge they can quickly activate and apply (Wassermann 1999). All day long, teachers make decisions about what to teach, whether a demonstration was effective, when to scaffold or support students' learning, how to respond to students' negative comments, what to say to a concerned parent, or what strategies to offer a child who can't retell a story or has difficulty selecting important information from a science textbook chapter.

Decision making is an integral part of teaching and according to Wassermann (1999), it requires three abilities:

- the ability to observe students, then compare observations to similar and different situations and to theoretical knowledge
- the ability to analyze the data collected from observations by selecting key points
- the ability to interpret these points by forming unconfirmed hypotheses or hunches that lead to informed action.

For example, a fourth grader starts sustained silent reading by announcing that reading is boring and dumb. He repeatedly spends the twenty minutes leafing through books that are far above his third-grade independent level, doodles, or turns the pages of sports magazines. Possible interpretations are that he is insecure about reading, has difficulty selecting appropriate books, can't concentrate, doesn't know how to personally connect to a book, can't visualize, has problems decoding multisyllabic words, lacks fluency, and so on. Because there were so many possibilities, the teacher decided to confer with the youngster, establish a relationship with the boy, collect and study data from school records, and speak to the student's former third-grade teacher before evaluating his knowledge and use of reading strategies.

3. What is an effective way for teachers to continue to learn while they are teaching?

   Response: Participating in a professional study group that responds to the diverse backgrounds and needs of teachers at a school is an ideal way to keep abreast of educational research and children's literature. Study groups also provide opportunities for teachers to exchange ideas, try new strategies, and obtain feedback on teaching practices.

Variations on a Theme

This sentence appears in the last chapter of *Living Between the Lines* (Calkins with Harwayne 1991): "If we as teachers are going to nurture our souls, we need each other" (303). Needing each other and nurturing our souls are two concepts that can drive study groups. A study group is one way of responding to the isolation teachers know well, for we work alone most of the day and crave opportunities to share concerns about a student or a strategy that worked or needs fine-tuning and discuss professional books and articles.

A study group can be organized in many ways as long as it meets monthly, bimonthly, or weekly. Teachers can receive graduate credit from a university or continuing-education or recertification units from their district, as long as the work completed meets guidelines set by state education departments. Here are some ways to organize study groups:

A faculty divides into small groups   Interest in a specific topic determines these groups.

Grade levels within a school learn together   When schools have eight to ten teachers in each grade, they often negotiate and study topics that are relevant to them. This permits members of grade-level teams to support one another.

Teachers from different schools learn together   Within one school district, teachers can select a school for their meetings. If study centers around a graduate class, teachers from different school districts can meet at the university that offers credit or at a school that is centrally located for all participants.

Effective study groups differ from the types of grouping that teachers may have experienced in traditional graduate courses. The chart that follows highlights these differences.

Study Group	Traditional Graduate Course
• Curriculum is negotiated: participants have input into what's studied.	• Syllabus contains a preplanned course fixed by university and state accreditation boards.
• Facilitator responds to teachers' needs.	• Professor controls content.
• Teachers learn by doing.	• Knowledge is delivered through lectures.
• Study is connected to Brian Cambourne's conditions of learning.	• Teachers learn by passively receiving information, reading, and taking notes.
• Experiences relate to the classroom and teachers' inquiries.	• Content is determined by syllabus.
• Small groups work together.	• Membership is large.
• Inquiry drives curriculum.	• Fixed topics drive curriculum.
• Frequency and length of meetings are negotiated.	• Frequency and length of meetings are determined by university credit hours.
• Goals are to improve teaching, improve students' learning, and enlarge theoretical base.	• Goals are to complete syllabus and enlarge theoretical knowledge.
• Assessment links what teachers learn about students to the kinds of learning experiences students receive.	• Assessment occurs through term papers and exams.

The study-group model responds to teachers and children, for teachers bring what they are learning to their students. The primary goal of all professional study is to improve children's learning, and study groups strive to do this. To weave study groups into the fabric of school life means we must create time.

Creating Time for Study Groups

Before schools organize study groups, administrators and teachers must establish priorities and make some decisions about how they use school time. Through collaboration, it's possible to save time and organize ongoing professional study.

In middle schools, grade-level teams usually have three to five common planning periods per week; teachers can set aside one or two of these forty-five-minute periods each month for professional study. Evan Robb, principal of Warren County Junior High School, has reserved time for department heads and/or teachers to lead study groups for one hour after school on two Thursday afternoons a month. At these meetings, teachers share learning strategies and discuss professional articles and students who are struggling. Evan, his assistant principal, and the dean of students rotate among the department meetings. Teachers read about administrative issues in newsletters.

On the other hand, most elementary school teachers don't have common planning times, and lunch is not the appropriate setting for serious study and reflection. Moreover, teachers spend long hours preparing effective lessons and reflecting on teaching practices.

Arriving at school early and leaving late, teachers plan lessons, grade papers, post student work on bulletin boards, review and reflect on students' work and teacher's observational notes to plan interventions that can support students' reading and writing, meet informally with colleagues, or tutor a student. Many have after-school family obligations and complete their work at home in the evening. Often, schools solve the issue of common time by reserving a one-hour faculty meeting each month for professional study; some set aside thirty minutes twice each month, devoting ten to twenty minutes to other issues. Faculty meeting time is ideal because it is part of the school schedule and a common time when teachers expect or are required to remain late one day each week.

Once schools reserve a faculty meeting for professional study, it's important to recognize that additional responsibilities have been placed on teachers and administrators. To dispense quickly with administrative issues and have time for study groups, administrators publish key items related to scheduling, visitors, new students, field trips, and so on several days prior to a faculty meeting. Instead of discussing these issues, teachers are then responsible for reading this information and following through on requests. Sometimes, it is necessary to poll the faculty on a key item at the meeting; completing this efficiently still allows time for study groups.

Time is a precious resource that schools should spend in ways that benefit all members of the community. Once a school sets aside time, the next challenge is to construct a climate that encourages professional study.

Conditions for Learning in Study Groups

In his book *The Whole Story: Natural Learning and the Acquisition of Literacy in the Classroom* (1988), Brian Cambourne documented what he observed in classrooms where young children were engaged in literacy learning. From his observations, Cambourne developed a list of seven conditions he believed were necessary for successful language acquisition.

It's my belief that these conditions are the same for children and adults. When learners construct knowledge, these conditions are present.

The following chart provides a summary of Cambourne's conditions and how these apply to the adult community of learners.

Cambourne's Conditions for Children	Learning Conditions for Adults
Immersion: Children must be surrounded by all kinds of print.	**Immersion:** Professional books, journal articles, and children's literature must be available to teachers in order for them to learn.
Demonstration: Students learn when teachers and peers demonstrate or model the structure and use of texts for reading and writing.	**Demonstration:** Teachers demonstrate for one another, presenting mini-lessons, reading-writing connections, and strategies. Sharing minilessons provides glimpses into colleagues' processes and augments background knowledge.

Expectation: Each class contains students at varied levels of expertise in reading, writing, thinking, and speaking. Based on past experiences at home and at school, all of these learners have their own expectations of what they can and cannot learn. When teachers set high expectations that students can reach, they can dramatically affect student performance, for as Cambourne notes, "Expectations are subtle and powerful coercers of behavior" (35).

Responsibility: Children learn best when they make decisions about when, what, and how to learn.

Use: Learners need time to practice and use their new knowledge in realistic and natural ways.

Approximation: Mistakes are necessary for learning to take place. A safe environment allows for mistakes as a natural way to know and understand.

Expectation: Our peer group will be as varied as the students are in our classrooms. A school's faculty is a mix of beginning, developing, and master teachers who can learn together as long as they value and respect what colleagues know.

Responsibility: Teachers share the responsibility of negotiating a study group's learning and assessment agenda with the facilitator.

Use: Teachers who have the time to practice and analyze strategies in study groups are more likely to risk trying them with students.

Approximation: Strategies learned and practiced during study groups don't always work the first time we try them with students. Study groups should be safe places where teachers can discuss unsuccessful learning experiences and colleagues can suggest adjustments.

Response: Feedback from and exchanges with more knowledgeable learners help children make meaning.

Response: Feedback validates what we are doing and provides support and suggestions for revising a lesson that derailed.

Reflection: The Eighth Condition for Learning

Reflection is teachers' guide for their decision-making process. In their article "Reflection Is at the Heart of Practice," Hole and McEntee (1999) write: "We all have a tendency to jump into an interpretive or a judgmental mode, but it is important to begin by simply telling the story" (35). The authors of this article invite teachers' to delay their desire to take action and move into a reflective mode by noting what happened, exploring all meanings, and then considering possible interventions and changes in teaching practices.

Deeply in touch with their own literacy processes, reflective teachers, as Donald Graves points out in *Discover Your Own Literacy* (1990), recognize that knowing themselves as learners can heighten their sensitivity to how students learn and to interpreting daily classroom events.

In addition to creating conditions for learning, another primary job of the study group's facilitator is to encourage teachers to think about their reading, shared demonstrations, and how a strategy worked in their classroom. Such reflection leads to a deeper knowledge and understanding of how theory and research translate into classroom learning events. Thinking can support the integration of personal experiences and theory, enabling teachers to evaluate and revise teaching and learning goals.

Study Group Facilitators

Choosing a facilitator is an important decision, and there is no single right way of selecting one (Birchak et al. 1998). Sometimes the facilitator is an outside consultant who visits a school once or twice a month or a consultant hired exclusively for facilitating study groups. Other times an administrator, the librarian, or a classroom teacher in a school guides the group. I have been a member of study groups in which the facilitator rotates, offering everyone an opportunity to steer the discussion. Being a facilitator is a challenge that includes taking risks, having experience and expertise in a specific topic, and possessing the self-discipline to observe and guide.

Some Guidelines for Facilitators

The primary goal of a facilitator is to help participants explore ideas relating to a topic, such as emergent literacy, without taking sides. These ideas can come from research, professional materials, and teachers' personal experiences. As an active listener, the facilitator repeats key points made by participants, summarizes the primary issues raised before the close of the meeting, and, with participants, negotiates the agenda for the next meeting. When the facilitator steps into a discussion as a participant, it should be brief, for the main purpose is to facilitate. Here are some additional guidelines for facilitators:

1. Begin the meeting on time and follow the agenda or plan negotiated with participants at the previous meeting.

2. Read the notes you took from the last meeting to refresh participants' minds.

3. Invite participants to share a minilesson, how a reading or writing strategy worked in their classroom, and so on.

4. Keep the discussion going with these questions: Does anyone have something to add? Does anyone have a different perspective? Can you offer research that supports this idea? Can you show us and interpret students' work? Can you elaborate on that idea? Can you clarify that point with an example from your classroom or from professional reading?

5. Encourage members to link and adapt theory, demonstrations, and discussions to their classrooms.

6. Help resolve heated disagreements by repeating the salient points each side raised and pointing out that diverse ideas can coexist.

7. Negotiate assignments for participants and the agenda for the next study group.

8. Write up the high points after the meeting on notebook paper or on forms your school has developed. Distribute these to appropriate persons.

Responsibilities of the Participants

The success of a study group depends upon the commitment of the participants to improve teaching and students' learning through shared study. Commitment means that once assignments and an agenda have been negotiated and agreed upon, the readings will be completed and teachers will prepare their presentations, participate in discussions, and raise thoughtful questions.

While facilitating a group of kindergarten and first-grade teachers who requested to study guided reading, it became obvious at the third meeting that no one had completed the assigned reading in *Guided Reading: Good First Teaching for All Children* (Fountas and Pinnell 1996). Immediately, I shared my feelings, for I have found that honesty quickly confronts the issue. "I sense that the readings for the last two sessions have not been done. Am I right?" I asked gently.

Comments like "I'm too busy," or "It's hard to find time when you have to share the book with two others," or "I didn't think it was *that* important" filled the room. The opportunity to vent can be positive as long as the group moves on to possible ways to solve the problem. This group solved the problem by asking the principal to purchase a book for each teacher. We agreed to extend the study group to one hour and fifteen minutes, using the first thirty minutes to complete the reading. Once teachers have negotiated a topic that's meaningful to them, the facilitator can usually mediate ways to continue moving forward.

Determining Study-Group Topics

In "Negotiating the Curriculum: Programming for Learning" (1992), Jon Cook discusses how teachers negotiate curriculum with students. The process, according to Cook, begins with raising questions: "What do we know now about a topic?" and "What do we want to know?" When teachers negotiate the content of study groups with one another, it's helpful to consider topics by posing these two questions.

Exploring topics teachers might want to study opens with free brainstorming. In groups of four to five, teachers discuss and record a list of ideas they want to investigate. Discovering and negotiating topics can occur at the beginning or the end of the year.

Negotiating Topics at Keister Elementary

It's early June, my last visit for the year at Keister Elementary School. Since next year I'll be coaching teachers in grades four and five, those teachers and I meet for one hour after school to explore possible topics for the monthly study groups I'll facilitate in the coming year. Ann Conners, principal, and Joe Nicholas, assistant principal, do not attend this meeting because they want teachers to create their agenda without feeling administrative pressure. Eight teachers divide into two groups and generate these ideas, which I record on large chart paper:

- supporting struggling readers
- supporting reluctant writers
- strategies that help students read difficult textbooks
- writing expository paragraphs
- book reviews
- writing poetry
- personal journals—how to make them more effective
- writers notebooks
- learning grammar through writing
- ways to respond to literature in journals
- grading journals so teachers are not overwhelmed
- word walls
- scheduling reading groups—organizing meaningful center work

Next, I ask teachers to prioritize the list and select the seven topics they want to investigate during the coming school year. Teachers rate them, using 7 for the most important topic and 1 for the least important. I tally the numbers, and teachers use these to select five topics that can be studied by small groups and/or the entire group of eight.

Supporting struggling readers and writers is the most pressing need of teachers. I initiate the study by posing Garth Boomer's questions and inviting groups to discuss these. One group noted that by talking about what they already know, they identified areas where they could support each other. This exercise also narrowed the focus of the two issues they selected:

- How can we help and motivate students who write little to expand their pieces and include details?
- How can we use reading strategies to help students improve?

The Importance of Negotiating

Inviting teachers to participate in choosing topics to be studied creates ownership of the commitment to learn and identifies the specific interests and concerns of a faculty, which vary from year to year and school to school. Reserving time to explore and then negotiate study-group topics affects teachers' attitudes and dedication to study in these ways:

- A community of learners dedicated to meaningful topics develops.
- A rough plan of the direction of the study emerges.
- Teachers discover one another's strengths and needs, and this opens the doors for continued communication and support.
- Curiosity increases from the desire to study a relevant topic.
- Prior knowledge and experiences have been activated.

The consultant's or school staff developer's goal is to provide clear experiences for organizing and continuing the momentum of study groups. Once teachers understand the process, they can organize and lead study groups without support from others. I recommend that teachers rotate the position of facilitator, offering volunteers the opportunity to guide the process.

After I have worked with them in study groups for a year, teachers at Keister have gained enough experience to continue the process without a consultant. They revisit the list of topics, add new ones, set priorities, question and discuss, and decide to rotate the role of facilitator.

Sometimes, no member of a faculty is knowledgeable about a topic, such as Vygotsky's theories of learning and social interaction. I view this as a great adventure, during which members of the group scaffold one another as they map untrod territory. Other times, a topic such as peer mediation or conflict-resolution requires more than a group effort. If the need is urgent, bring it to the attention of the administration and lobby for the school to hire an expert who can train teachers.

A Framework for Study Groups

Since the goal of study groups is to improve teaching and students' learning, I developed a structure that links what's studied to the classroom. In writing and reading workshop (Calkins with Harwayne 1991; Graves 1994; Harwayne 1992; Hindley 1996; Robb 1999), students share their work to collect feedback from peers and to advertise diverse ways of adapting reading strategies and writing techniques. The study groups I lead bring the following workshop model to professional study.

1. The session opens with teachers sharing a strategy studied during the last meeting or one they discovered from their own professional reading. Teachers share minilessons recorded on charts that they developed to introduce the strategy, share samples of students' work, and learn from one another. I always spotlight and celebrate what worked. Once teachers feel safe, many present lessons that posed problems and ask the group for feedback and suggestions.

2. Members sum up, highlighting what worked for them and posing questions about areas that need clarification.

3. Next, I divide the professional reading the group agreed to complete at the previous meeting into sections for pairs and/or small groups to skim. The group chooses someone to teach the salient points of its section. Often, I add related comments from my experience and reading.

4. I present a minilesson and think-aloud and actively involve the group in a research-based strategy or technique.

5. Participants question one other and me.

6. I provide articles for the group to read as well as a chapter from a book the school purchased.

7. Between meetings, teachers try a new strategy and continue to read professional articles.

I've applied this structure to three kinds of study groups: those that meet at Powhatan, where I teach, groups that meet at schools where I coach, and groups working for graduate credit from a university.

What a Study Group Discussion Sounds Like

Topic: Vocabulary

Study-Group Members: Dick Bell, history teacher, Mary Hofstra, reading specialist, Harry Holloway, math teacher, Laura Robb, reading-writing workshop teacher, Nancy Roche, third-grade teacher

Rotating Facilitator: Today, Dick is the facilitator.

Professional Reading: Chapter 9, pp. 197–212 in *Reading and Reasoning Beyond the Primary Grades* (Vaughan and Estes 1986)

Presentation: Mary Hofstra, "Finding Context Clues"

Summary of Meeting Up to the Discussion: Harry showed the group the bulletin boards his sixth graders were setting up in the library. Topics were triangles, polygons, quadrilaterals, and circles. Each group posted a list of vocabulary words necessary for their topic, and group members introduced their vocabulary to the class using models, constructions, and hands-on experiences, such as making polygons or different types of triangles.

After the group discussed the pages read in Chapter 9 of *Reading and Reasoning Beyond the Primary Grades,* Mary presented a vocabulary lesson on using context clues to figure out tough words that she modeled for fourth graders.

Excerpt from the Groups' Discussion

Dick: How did the students work on these examples?

Mary: With a partner, so they could help one another.

Harry: Do you always have students pick their own words?

Mary: Sometimes I select words before they read and we do a "predict and clarify" in groups of four.

Nancy: How does that strategy work?

Mary: I give students four to five words, and on a sheet, the group makes predictions using their knowledge of roots, prefixes, and if they think they've met this word before. Then, students read the sentences surrounding each word and start to clarify their predictions. As we read, reread, and discuss the text, students continue to clarify their original predictions using context clues.

Harry: I think that strategy would work well with a chapter in math that had some unfamiliar words.

Dick: I've tried it in history, and students really recall the meanings because they are the ones clarifying explanations. I find that sharing their clarifications helps them remember even more.

Laura: With the class, or in their groups?

Dick: I use both, depending on whether I feel that students need to hear all their classmates' ideas. But let's focus on context clues today. How can these strategies help students?

Nancy: They can figure out words while they are reading and not stop the flow of the story to ask for help.

Harry: They'll be able to deal with unknown words in passages on standardized tests.

Mary: Finding the time is so difficult, but this is important.

Laura: You might want to try working on vocabulary in context for ten minutes, three to four times a week.

Dick: With older students, that works better. I lose them if I continue for the period.

Harry: Last week, we discussed how important it was to connect students' prior knowledge to a new word. This strategy doesn't do that.

Mary: I encourage students to try to make connections to similar words and past experiences as they exchange how they clarified a word.

Harry: That's a good idea. I think it's important for all of us to tell our students, again and again, how linking a new word to what they already know about it can help them remember the meaning.

The vitality of study groups resides in the questions that members raise, and the way teachers from diverse grade levels probe a strategy to deepen their knowledge of how it can help their students.

Professional Study at Powhatan

Several years ago, John Lathrop, Head of Powhatan, asked me to create a staff development plan for teachers. John set aside one seventy-five-minute faculty meeting a month for professional study.

During the first two years, the faculty chose to review reading strategies, writing workshop, and research curricula. Teachers created a K–8 overview for each area, then studied and revised the document. Every other year we revisit and adjust these overviews; adjustments grow out of teachers' personal experiences and professional reading. Reading these books shaped the faculty's thinking and stimulated thought-provoking discussions during several meetings: *What Research Has to Say About Reading Instruction,* edited by Samuels and Farstrup (1992) and *Guided Reading: Good First Teaching For All Children* (1996) and *Word Matters: Teaching Phonics and Spelling in the Reading/Writing Classroom* (1998), both by Fountas and Pinnell. The third year, the faculty chose to revisit writing workshop.

Faculty Letter-Writing Partnerships

My goal for teachers was to have them better understand the writing process through an authentic experience. That's why, in addition to reading articles from two NCTE Journals, *Primary Voices* and *Voices in the Middle,* teachers chose to read *A Fresh Look at Writing* by Donald Graves (1994) or Ralph Fletcher's *What a Writer Needs* (1993). To help teachers understand the writing process, I invited pairs of teachers to write letters to each other.

At a meeting, we thoroughly discussed the proposed project, and teachers who wanted to participate requested that chance determine their partners. Teachers who agreed to correspond received this invitation:

Dear Powhatan Colleagues,

I hope that all of you will accept the invitation to correspond with a faculty partner each month. Partners will negotiate time frames so that letters are available for voluntary sharing at monthly meetings.

By writing letters to one another, we will all be engaged in writing that goes beyond notes, messages, and brief journal entries. Since learning is in the "doing," and since all of us use writing in our classes, I thought letters would be a useful form to deepen our understanding of the process cycle. I believe that in order to convincingly talk about and demonstrate technique, parts of the process cycle, and our feelings toward writing, we must engage in writing at a meaningful and challenging level.

In your letters you can write about articles we read and discuss, books partners agree to read together, and stories about your students and your life. These letters should be rich in detail and move deeply into beliefs and feelings. Please save your notes and drafts, and the final piece to be delivered and responded to during the weeks between sessions.

Lois Lowry believes, and I agree, that letter writing is a wonderful way to share personal stories, vent feelings, and discuss books and movies. Lowry corresponds with several authors and with her two daughters who live nearby. "In writing to them," she notes, "I heighten my senses and generate an excitement for writing. Letter writing makes me think and motivates me to do other writing."

As we correspond, we will talk about our process, and I will continue to model various ways to talk about writing with the children.

Issuing an invitation means accepting the fact that some teachers will not participate, and out of twenty teachers and teaching assistants, six pairs corresponded. To discover their partner, teachers drew names from a paper bag.

Teachers' Correspondence

The following selections from teachers' correspondence reveal teachers' honesty, their struggles with writing, a willingness to discuss school issues, a collaborative spirit, and an enjoyment of exchanging personal experiences and feelings. The first pair of ideas were exchanged between second-grade teacher Carol Chapman and history and Latin teacher Dick Bell.

Dear Dick,

It is ridiculous that this letter is so difficult for me to write. In my self-evaluation, I find I lack a great deal of confidence in my writing. I do realize the difficulty that children must feel when they write and share. Although, the children continue to amaze me as they beg to have "author's chair" and read to the class everything they have written.

Also, there is a movement to have twenty-four students in the sixth, seventh, and eighth grade classes. How do you feel about that? How will it affect your teaching? Is it too big a jump from eighteen?

I feel a sense of relief and some accomplishment as I reread this letter and am almost certain that I will deliver it to your mailbox today. (I do feel under some pressure since we are again meeting with Laura today!) Thanks for your patience.

Your friend,

Carol

Dear Carol,

I greatly enjoyed your letter. Like you I am petrified to have my writing publicly aired, but I'm working hard at dealing with my feelings. It does humble me to be writing to you and makes me think about the expectations I have for students. Sometimes they're not reasonable, and I'm asking students to do too much too quickly.

How do I feel about twenty-four in a class? In English and history you'll have to shorten the curriculum because of workshop where we work with groups and do lots of individual conferences. Also, we encourage our students to ask lots of questions about minilessons and books and their writing. I'm not sure we can meet with as many students with six more in a class. For the kids, it's great as it means more social contacts and choices for friendships. Let's keep writing and talking about this.

Have you thought about doing a cross-grade project with my seventh graders? Let's meet at lunch one day next week and see if we can generate some ideas. Also, let's invite our students to brainstorm suggestions and compare lists.

Dick

The next exchange took place between Harry Holloway, a mathematics teacher, and me.

Dear Laura,

I need to create agendas for the next few eighth grade class meetings. Any ideas?

Any chance of us doing some classes together? How about seventh grade math on Mondays at 11:15? I don't have any writing planned right now, but I have several projects waiting in the wings. Before we do a technical writing assignment with kids, it would be a good idea if we agreed on what we want.

Math 8 will be putting stuff up on the hall bulletin board, so you will see some of the things we are doing. There is still so much to do with this class. I am going to try to create some folders for independent studies for students who can move ahead. This way I can work with those who are struggling now.

On another note, an eighth grader who is in my advisement group, expressed a desire to improve her handwriting. Who at school would have some time and knowledge to work with her and find out what she needs? I'm sure that with help, we can find resources that can improve her handwriting. But we need someone who can follow through, not just sporadic meetings.

Harry

Dear Harry,

I do want to do technical writing with you. Why don't I reserve a Wednesday or Thursday English period in mid-January that will give us time to meet and plan? Another reason for waiting until mid-January is that the eighth grade needs all the time I can give them to complete their author studies. They are having a difficult time meeting deadlines set over several weeks. Most are used to completing assignments the evening before they are due. Budgeting time, and reflecting on how long parts of a project will take, is something all of us need to work on with them.

Back to technical writing. It would be great to have students write on something—we can discuss options—and have them test their writing on another class. The distance and objectivity of another grade will enable them to see, even more clearly, the pluses and pitfalls of their thinking. We might even make progress! The class that tests the eighth graders' work can learn how to write clear and objective comments and questions that our students can use to revise.

I've given much thought to possible topics for eighth grade class meetings. Since I'm always reluctant to provide topics, I'm suggesting that you have students work in pairs and brainstorm lists of topics they'd like to discuss. You can read the lists, select ten to fifteen for them to prioritize, and you'll have more topics than you can cover. I know that you are sensitive to students' lives, so that if an event occurs that needs discussing, you'll set aside the planned agenda that day.

The Anno books you gave me are fascinating. Those are wonderful picture books to start with—I'd love to see teams of eighth graders create their own problem solving texts. I'm intrigued by the notion of pictures as a way into mathematical concepts. Let's talk about doing this as a joint venture.

Laura

Response to Letter Writing

All participants loved receiving mail. Everyone agreed that the physical act of committing ideas to paper involved more thought and planning than dashing off an e-mail. Conscious of the fact that a letter has more permanence than e-mail, many wrote first and second drafts before delivering them.

Some partners continued their correspondence after the school year ended. Participants agreed that letter writing forced them to reflect on their own writing process and deepened their empathy toward students who struggled to write, because often the teachers struggled to express ideas. Moreover, teachers used their struggles to explore ways to support students' writing process. "I told students I'd make lists of what I was trying to say, then pick items to include in my letter," said Carol Chapman. "This became a minilesson, and I'd share my list and part of the letter."

Record Keeping: Documenting Meetings

In June, after evaluating letter writing, teachers brainstormed a list of fifteen topics for next year's professional study. Organizing small groups that would study together during monthly professional study meetings was a logical solution to meeting the faculty's range of needs.

Powhatan teachers narrowed a list of fifteen suggested topics to six: computers and technology in the classroom, vocabulary, word walls, library resources, and foreign language instruction. It's important each year to brainstorm a new list of topics, for as teachers grow, what they wish to study changes. Next, negotiate the number of meetings to set aside during the year for small-group study.

Study groups can meet several times or for most of the year. Whatever scheduling framework you negotiate, reserve two meetings at the end of the year for groups to share their learning and respond to queries from colleagues.

At our first gathering in September, I helped Powhatan's faculty establish a structure for meetings. Keeping records, we agreed, would enable groups to accurately share what they learned with everyone, and we developed a goal and debriefing sheet and a summary sheet (see Appendix D).

The first form reminded groups of the guidelines they set and asked the group members to set goals and debrief one another at the close of their meeting, listing what worked and what could be improved. My hope was that insights gained from debriefings would be applied to future meetings.

On the second form, groups listed the members who attended and noted what the group discussed. Everyone decided that groups could select one facilitator or rotate that position.

The excerpts of records from the vocabulary and word wall group that follow illustrate the detailed notes members kept and also reveal that teachers did try new instructional strategies. Groups placed a copy of their records in my mailbox, and I kept them in a folder in my office and encouraged teachers to read one another's.

Goal and Debriefing Record

- Before starting, establish goals for each one-hour session.
- If it's necessary to read materials between staff development meetings, work with the group to achieve consensus.
- To integrate new ideas into your teaching practices, it is crucial to try these in your classes. Teachers can select one thing to try in their classes and quickly share at the next meeting. It is also helpful if teachers photocopy samples of some students' work and bring these to the group.
- Reserve five minutes at the end of each session to debrief. First ask teachers to discuss what worked, then offer some suggestions for improvement.

Goals: Vocabulary Group   **Date:** April 10

Presentations: (1) KWL (approach to) vocabulary; (2) preteaching key words in science

Assignment: (3) Try one of these in your class.

Debriefing:

What Worked	*Needs*
• modeling beforehand how to use affixes, roots, and sentence content to deduce meaning	• use only a few words per chapter in science—three to five
• putting page number by words so kids could skim and reread	• use words for sorting
• working collaboratively— *kids need to work together— they'll get more ideas and help slower learners*	• develop a list of synonyms and antonyms

---

Summary Sheet for Study Groups

Date: September

List members attending:

Carol, Nancy, Mary [Jennifer, Jenny, Jo, and Robin on field trip]

List books and/or articles you are using as resources:

- *Phonics They Use: Words For Reading and Writing,* 2d edition by P. Cunningham (1995).
- *Words Their Way: Word Study for Phonics, Vocabulary and Spelling Instruction* by Bear, Invernizzi, Johnston, Templeton (1996).

Summarize, in a list or paragraph, what you covered:

1. Group members should observe word walls in classes at our school and other schools.
2. Type of word wall discussed: high frequency.
3. Word wall activities can be done during guided reading: word ladders or stairs; children read word wall; try to write a sentence with word wall words; pairs say words on wall.

Goal(s) for next meeting:

Add five words per week to the wall.

Assignment:

Read about a word wall activity, try it, and bring to October meeting.

Specialized Study Groups

In addition to organizing yearly study groups, I have invited teachers who have expertise in specific areas to plan professional study sessions. On the school calendar are ten professional study meetings. We divide into small study groups for six of the ten meetings. The remaining four are whole-group meetings led by teachers.

The entire faculty receives a list of suggested study groups and teacher-led sessions to choose from. Hands-on workshops led by teachers have included guided reading, book talks on new library acquisitions, problem solving, using the Internet for research, and reading strategies across the curriculum.

Powhatan Teachers Evaluate Study Groups

At our last faculty meeting of the year, I obtained reactions to study groups by posing two questions: (1) What do I think of the concept of study groups? (2) Did participation affect your teaching? How?

The responses that follow celebrate the benefits of including small study groups in a school's professional development program.

> Splitting into groups was a good idea. It gave us the time to think more deeply about the subjects we teach, the way we teach, and what could be improved.
>
> It gave me the motivation to put some ideas into practice and experiment. It worked and I'm glad I did it.
>
> —*French teacher Fabienne Modesitt*

> I loved sharing what I do and hearing what others do. Our project motivated me to create a word study game, use it in the classroom and get "kid feedback." This group was loosely structured. Perhaps next time we should use more structure and have more time.
>
> I will continue to work in word study in my room, but I have a lot to learn. One of the best ways is to try a new strategy, and if it is successful, according to me and the children, use it. If not, adjust the strategy or try something else.
>
> —*Second-grade teacher Carol Chapman*

> I enjoyed being in the vocabulary group. It was important for me to have a choice. I found the sessions thought-provoking and interesting. It was helpful to see how others used strategies similar to ones I used. I tried two collaborative vocabulary strategies with my classes, and students enjoyed working together. Returning to the group for feedback and suggestions helped me and my students.
>
> —*History and Latin teacher Dick Bell*

Fifteen teachers felt that setting aside additional faculty meeting time for study groups would be more helpful to them. However, this seems unlikely to happen, since it would mean scheduling additional after-school meetings to discuss students' progress, a topic that is also important.

Study Groups at Other Schools

When I spend one day a month at a school and close that day with a one-hour study group, I work with one or two grade levels, the reading specialists, ESL teachers who support these grades, and administrators. Group members select topics from a long list they compiled in June relevant to their grade and student population. During meetings, the whole group breaks into smaller groups to present information in professional articles and books. A strong connection exists between study-group topics, teaching practices, and what I am invited to observe and/or demonstrate during my visit. These links support teachers as they try new strategies to improve students' learning.

Sandy Palmer, a fourth-grade teacher at Keister Elementary School, shared the following journal entry with me. Though not required to attend the second/third-grade study group, Sandy participated in several sessions to "expand my knowledge of specific topics." Intensely interested in word walls, Sandy worked with the group and read *Word Matters: Teaching Phonics and Spelling in the Reading/Writing Classroom* by Fountas and Pinnell (1998). Her study directly affected her teaching, as this journal entry illustrates.

Journal
March
Word Walls

I instituted a new strategy in my classroom this year. I wanted to provide a place for all of the rich vocabulary that is taught, discovered, and learned across the content areas over the course of a year at school.

In my classroom I have four closet doors that are covered with bulletin board paper. Each one has a banner of writing at the top. They read:

- Words Readers and Writers Use
- Words Scientists Use
- Words Social Scientists and Historians Use
- Words Mathematicians Use

Over the course of this year, words have been added to the walls as the children discover their importance. We have had discussions about the appropriate placement of words like "data," which fall under both math and science. And most beneficial of all, the words are there for students' reference—for spelling, meaning, and reference.

Each student approaches the wall differently—meaning that some use it for spelling purposes while others for generating words for Latin and Greek roots in word study. The walls provide a level of accountability for my students—because the rule is if the word is on the wall, they need to know its meaning, its connection to the content area, and its importance to their learning.

Perhaps the utmost value I have witnessed is my students making connections between the vocabulary they are learning in one content area to other subjects. Because the word walls are cumulative, students are able to connect prior and more recent learning.

Second-grade teacher Faye Hastings worked with me on improving students' brainstorming, generating questions to gather more details for writing, and self-editing. Often, support and opportunities to exchange ideas with a coach or experienced peer enables a teacher to risk trying new strategies. Here is an excerpt from Faye's journal:

May 9

I'd like to share some reflections on what I've gained this year under your guidance, Laura. . . . You have also encouraged me to tackle exciting and difficult tasks.

I especially appreciate how my students have improved in revising. The class loves to meet with a partner in the prewriting stage to orally think through a story. I hear them asking each other questions for clarification as well as comments about specific parts of the story. I love the use of sticky notes to write my questions to the writers about their stories. Students have been careful, for the most part, to keep these communications.

Another improvement this year is students' self-editing and editing with a partner. Students take this editing seriously and really enjoy working with different partners. I give them one thing at a time to search for, and they continue to improve.

This type of journal entry celebrates teachers as learners and risk takers, and the beneficiaries of their commitment to grow are the children they teach. Since I make keeping journals optional because of the time involved, not all teachers in a study group keep journals. All members, however, share at the beginning of each meeting.

These share sessions and the questions and discussions that follow help me and others gain additional insights into a strategy. Sometimes, a first-year teacher like Jeff Nolt takes a strategy in a new direction. Jeff decided to try bookmarks with his fourth graders. Bookmarks, an idea developed by Dorothy Watson and described by Linda Crafton (1991), is a self-monitoring reading-response strategy that encourages readers to interact with texts. On a bookmark, which is a blank piece of paper folded in half lengthwise, students note their name, the title and author of the book, and the page or pages they're responding to. As they read, students stop every four to six pages and predict, question, agree, disagree, make personal connections, or note a confusing word. I recommended using the strategy to monitor whether students apply strategies practiced in class. Jeff kept a log of students' reactions to his modeling and practice sessions and students' reactions to their books.

Though many students disliked the bookmark strategy because self-monitoring their reading was difficult, Lizzy was one of those who enjoyed it. Jeff wrote

It had been a long time since I read *Catwings* [Ursula Le Guin 1998] but by perusing Lizzy's bookmark and skimming the text, I was quickly refreshed. We discussed her question, "p. #17, What is a pinnacle?" We hunted the sentence together, used context clues and the illustrations, and arrived at a definition. Lastly, I asked Lizzy to tell me her thoughts on the bookmark strategy, and she told me that she liked thinking about what she was reading this way. In four minutes, our conference was complete, and I was calling another student to our classroom library. (See Figures 6–1a and 6–1b.)

During our study-group meeting, Jeff read the last part of his entry: "I appreciate that bookmarks helped me avoid general questions at conferences. Instead of asking, 'What is this book about?' I can ask specific questions about details that might not come up in a conference without bookmarks. Also, I like the fact that bookmarks encourage students to become actively involved in their reading. This strategy had good results for me as a teacher and my students as learners." Jeff's risk taking showed me and his colleagues at Keister yet another way to use this effective strategy with students.

Earning University Credit Through Study Groups

When Nikki Isherwood, Director of Instruction for Winchester City Schools, asked me to create a reading-writing class for teachers in grades five to eight, I knew that I wanted to work with a small number of teachers using the study-group structure discussed on pages 87–94. Nikki Isherwood arranged for all teachers who enrolled in the class to receive graduate credit from an area university.

I limit enrollment to fifteen teachers, and I negotiate the content of the class, which centers around reading and writing. Small numbers allow full participation at each meeting. Classes have focused on primary-, elementary-, or middle-grade teachers; two included teachers in grades three to seven. Because a three-credit class meets twice each month for nine months, and classes are two and a half hours long, there's time for discussions, reflection, and studying professional books and journals. When teachers exchange their experiences with a strategy, they have countless opportunities to question, analyze, reflect, provide feedback for one another, and improve their own self-evaluative abilities.

Joan Johnson, veteran first-grade teacher at Quarles Elementary, was not quite sure that drawing pictures as a writing plan could improve first-grade

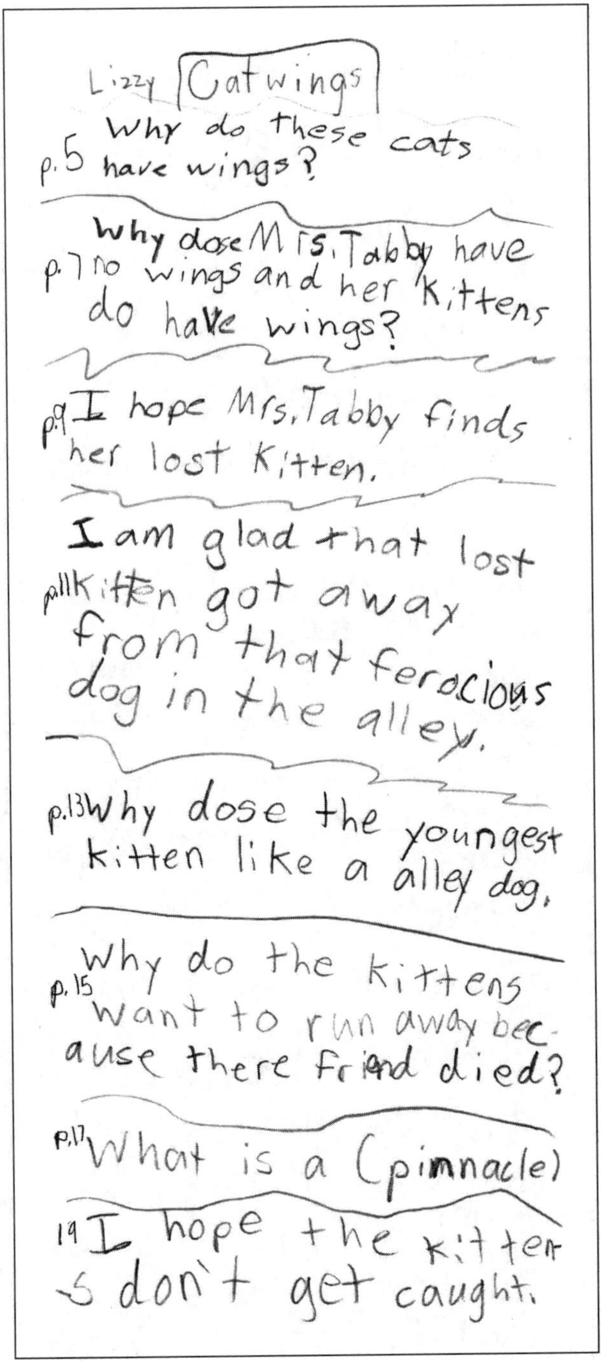

Lizzy [Catwings]

p.5 Why do these cats have wings?

p.7 Why dose Mrs.Tabby have no wings and her kittens do have wings?

p.9 I hope Mrs.Tabby finds her lost Kitten.

p.11 I am glad that lost kitten got away from that ferocious dog in the alley.

p.13 Why dose the youngest kitten like a alley dog.

p.15 Why do the kittens want to run away because there friend died?

p.17 What is a (pimnacle)

p.19 I hope the kittens don't get caught.

Figure 6–1a. Lizzy's bookmarks

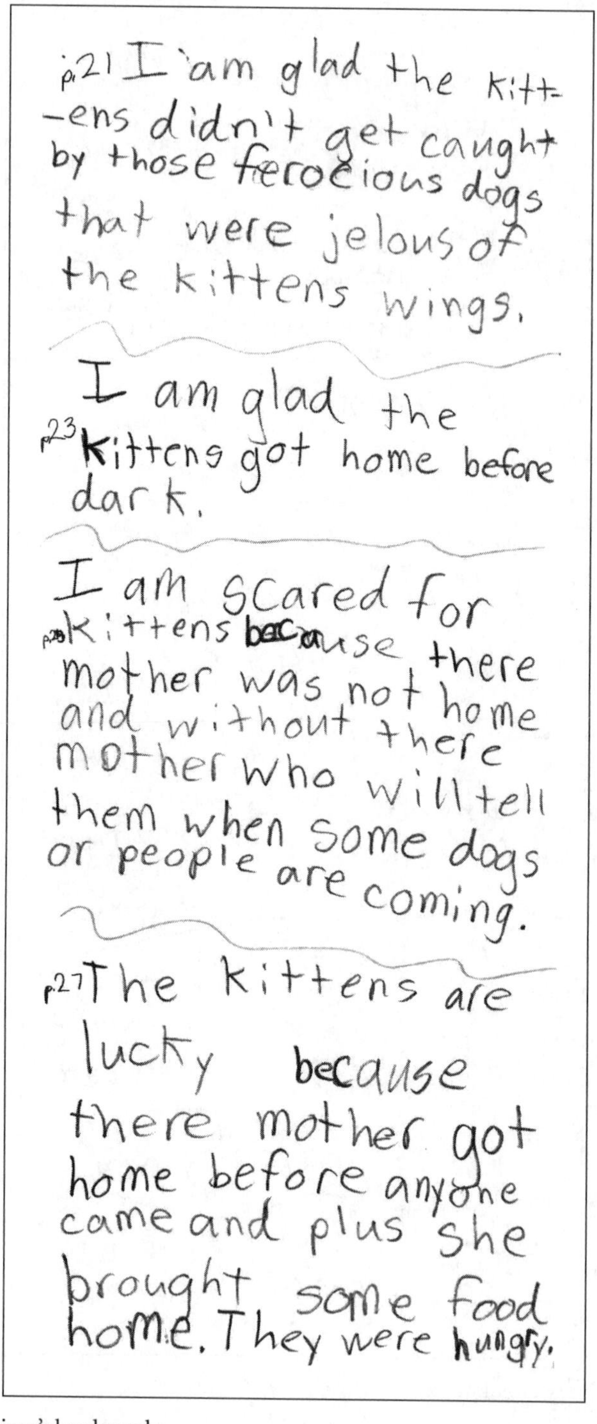

p21 I am glad the kitt-
-ens didn't get caught
by those ferocious dogs
that were jelous of
the kittens wings.

I am glad the
p23 kittens got home before
dark.

I am scared for
p25 kittens because there
mother was not home
and without there
mother who will tell
them when some dogs
or people are coming.

p27 The kittens are
lucky because
there mother got
home before anyone
came and plus she
brought some food
home. They were hungry.

Figure 6–1b. Lizzy's bookmarks

writers who said, "I have nothing to write." Joan's strategy was to confer with these students and help them generate ideas. However, time for several one-on-one conferences was not always available each week. Joan agreed to introduce the drawing strategy in her class and bring results to our next class. In a journal, Joan noted, "Shyanne's writing is very limited without my guidance" (see Figure 6–2, a piece Shyanne wrote without a plan). The writing-plan

Figure 6–2. Shyanne's writing without a picture plan

drawings (see Figure 6–3) resulted in her first organized composition: the first shows the pumpkin patch; the second, the carved pumpkin; and the third, the carved pumpkin in a tank. Shyanne's writing plan stayed on her desk as she wrote her story (see Figure 6–4). "Two weeks later, without a drawing," Joan writes, "Shyanne returned to a one-sentence story."

It was more difficult to convince teachers in third to fifth grade that drawings can improve writing. The teachers and I studied fourth graders' drawings of the beginning, middle, and end of pieces as well as the writing that emerged from these plans, discussing students' process and progress. Third-grade teacher Laurie Grey agreed to try this strategy. Selections from her journal illustrate Laurie's doubts, adaptations, and successes and her ability to take risks and learn from students.

We went to the pumpkin patch.

Figure 6–3a. Shyanne's picture plan

We carved a pumpkin.

Figure 6–3b. Shyanne's picture plan (*continued*)

10/11

I'm not convinced that drawing will improve my students' writing. Besides, in third grade, we're supposed to have students write with words and not use drawings like they did in K and 1.

10/15

Saw writing plans and pieces Laura brought in. What really impressed me was the difference between pieces with no plan—just one or two sentences.

11/3

Had students plan their writing using the beginning-middle-end writing plan. I decided not to demonstrate first, just wanted to see what they

We put the pumpkin on a table.

Figure 6–3c. Shyanne's picture plan (*continued*)

would do with the plan. Students brainstormed story ideas first. Most illustrated, some wrote captions, and several used bubbles to show characters speaking. Many drew similar pictures for all three sections, and it was difficult to tell what the events of the story would be.

11/12

Today I demonstrated how I would plan my story using the writing plan. I told students about the story I had in mind, brainstormed on a chart, and stressed the events took place over a whole day. When I drew pictures, I showed a clear difference from morning or beginning, to afternoon or middle, to night at the end. I explained that their stories did not have to cover a day, but that their pictures had to show a middle and an end that were different from the beginning. I also wrote a caption to explain each of my pictures, and suggested they do the same.

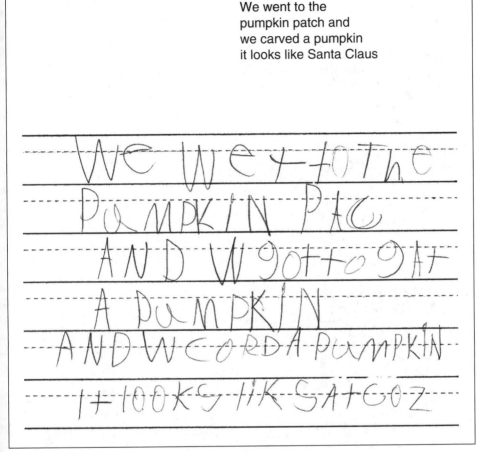

We went to the
pumpkin patch and
we carved a pumpkin
it looks like Santa Claus

Figure 6–4. Shyanne's writing with a picture plan

Results were better. Many students copied my idea of morning to night, but their illustrations showed more detail and their captions explained their pictures. I had students share their stories aloud, using their writing plans to guide them. Many wrote details in the captions that weren't in the illustrations. Others had more details in the pictures than the captions. Often, students expanded their stories as they spoke. I shared these observations and gave students time to add more to their plans.

11/19

Students were excited to write their stories. I didn't focus on spelling, grammar, or punctuation, just encouraged them to write from their plans. Students shared their stories with each other and we compared these to their writing plans. I hope that some students who stuck closely to their

Figure 6–5. Justin's writing plan

Justin
Language Arts
May 12, 1999

Tamy, Matt and Been ran away from home to the forest on October 8, 1996. Tamy was 9 years old at the time and the boys were both 10 years old. They were hungry so they looked inside the basket for food. But they did not see anything. Next they tried to take there hungry little minds off food by canoeing in a near by river. It did not work so they looked for food as good as KFC's (Kentucky Fried Chicken) chicken. When they found some juicy berries like an orange, they could not wait til they ate. At this point Tamy the youngest person in the family died with hunger. Finaly thay sat down and ate their food by the fire they tought of Tamy alot so.... They ran like a tiger runny for its prey in the jungle all the way home they hugged thier parents and said, We are sorry about Tamy.

Figure 6–6. Justin's story

plan began to see how they could expand their writing. (See Figures 6–5 and 6–6 for one student's plan and story.)

Laurie asked students to evaluate writing from a plan. All agreed that it was easier to write because the ideas were in front of them. Also, thinking about whether a story worked before starting helped them know if it had a beginning, middle, and end. After Laurie's presentation, others tried this strategy. Middle school teachers agreed that the drawing enabled reluctant writers and learning-disabled students to experience more success during writing workshop.

Closing Thoughts

Had anyone told me in August that I would enjoy a class from 4:00 to 6:30 that met twice a month for most of the year, I would have been amused. This reading and writing class was both fascinating and practical. Fascinating because we saw how others translated strategies and practical because strategies applied to what students needed. . . . The assignments—to try what we had learned in class and bring back the results to share were very doable. We had to try something new, something veteran teachers are loathe to do.

This excerpt from sixth-grade teacher Gretchen Saunders' evaluation of our graduate-credit study group sums up the benefits of negotiated study. When teachers study, collaborate, share, and reflect, they can enlarge their theory base, translate theory into practice, and receive beneficial feedback that continues to propel teachers and students forward.

7

Breaking Tradition
Teacher Evaluation as Professional Study

Teacher evaluation can be positive, empowering teachers to continue to grow, or it can be an anxiety-building event that focuses on what went wrong. Recently, a teacher with five years of experience called me after receiving her evaluation. It was obvious that she was trying to hold back tears, for her voice cracked and there were several long silences. Even though this young teacher felt that her fifth year had been her best, she told me that in five areas, the principal marked her lower than on her third-year evaluation. One area was dress, and this perplexed the teacher because with more salary, she was able to purchase several suits and dresses. What upset this teacher is that her evaluation was based on two visits from her principal. I urged her to speak to her principal and bring all of her evaluations to the meeting. "Ask him to explain the change and find out what you need to do," I counseled.

The outcome of this event is not significant. What is significant is that throughout the country, principals are fortunate if they can observe teachers three to four times. This system frustrates principals as much as teachers. I sympathize with principals of schools with more than one thousand students and a large staff to monitor. Often, it's difficult to even schedule two teacher observations a year. An evaluation of a teacher's performance based on two out of 180 days is akin to the standardized tests students and adults take to measure achievement and potential. In addition to mandated evaluations, in which all teachers are measured against uniform standards, I propose that schools develop performance-based assessment that encourages teacher growth and provides deep insights into teachers' performance and students' progress.

In this chapter, I will explain the nontraditional, performance-based peer-evaluation strategy that colleagues and I developed at Powhatan School.

Not meant to replace traditional teacher evaluation or regular classroom visits from administrators, this program can transform evaluation into professional study, for it encourages growth and change through the interactions between a teacher and peer evaluator.

Powhatan's Teacher-Evaluation Program

Halfway through John Lathrop's first year as Head of Powhatan, he challenged the faculty to explore teacher-evaluation options that kindled growth and improvement. "Simply telling teachers that their lesson didn't work is not enough," he told us. "Teachers require continuous follow up and support if positive change is to occur," he added. John asked me to chair a committee of three teachers, and he challenged us to formulate an innovative and inexpensive teacher-evaluation system that tapped the diverse strengths of our faculty. Reading specialist Mary Hofstra, third-grade teacher Nancy Roche, and sixth- and seventh-grade math teacher Harry Holloway volunteered.

Three meetings later, we proposed the following format at a full faculty meeting, inviting everyone to edit and adjust the proposal. Administrators could not participate as peer evaluators, for they had their own evaluation instruments. At Powhatan, since I am a member of the teaching staff, I serve as a peer evaluator.

Proposal for Evaluation as Professional Growth

- Every five years, teachers at Powhatan will be evaluated by a peer.
- The teacher invites a peer to participate in the yearlong evaluation.
- The peer has the right to turn down the invitation. Acceptance means a yearlong commitment to a process that starts and ends in June.
- The peer evaluator meets with the teacher to establish goals and for follow-up conversations after each written observation.
- Peer evaluators observe teachers six to eight times during a school year.
- The school will supply substitute teachers so peers can complete observations.
- Peer evaluators will suggest professional articles and books and teaching resources to teachers they are evaluating.
- The peer evaluator documents the first meeting and all formal classroom observations (see Appendix E).
- The teacher receives a copy of each formal observation and confers with the peer evaluator. On the observation form, the evaluator writes a summary of the conference.

Adjustments to the Original Proposal

At end-of-the-year faculty meetings, teachers adjust the evaluation-as-growth process. It's crucial to revisit the process and fine-tune it annually, for each year we experience the process, we can pinpoint areas that didn't work well and add ideas that did not occur to us before. The following are the adjustments to the original proposal.

- Evaluation of a teacher will occur every four years.
- The head of Powhatan as well as the lower and upper school heads will meet and generate a list of teachers who will be evaluated during the upcoming year. Teachers will learn this in May, so they have time to invite a peer evaluator.
- Visits should be negotiated with the teacher.
- The evaluator should circulate among students and support them.
- The peer evaluator will formally write up six to eight evaluations. To put students at ease, it's recommended that the peer evaluator visit two to three times prior to starting formal observations (see Appendix E).
- Observations and evaluations should relate to the goals set by the teacher and peer.
- Observations should cover an entire lesson and might require that the peer evaluator remain for a block of time.
- The peer evaluator will complete a summary form (see Appendix E) and submit these to John Lathrop. (John prefers reading an overview of the year instead of dozens of observations.)
- The peer evaluator will submit the goal and observation forms to the head of lower or upper school.
- The teacher will receive a copy of all write-ups.

If the evaluator is not proactive in arranging meetings and classroom visits, then the teacher must be responsible for putting the process into action. The process asks a high level of commitment from both, but the results—improved teaching and student learning—affect the pair. The goals established during the first meeting can and do change as partners investigate, confer, and learn throughout the year.

Snapshots of First Meetings

Since goal-setting meetings occur before the school year starts, I find these more relaxed and leisurely than the post-observation conferences scheduled during the year. Usually, the teacher and I reserve one to two hours for these first meetings that provide an opportunity for the teacher to talk about his or her philosophy and show me portfolios and reading and writing folders from past years. Out of this exchange emerge tentative goals that I record on a form (see Appendix E) and that we review and adjust throughout the year. As a peer evaluator, I explain that changing and adding goals is part of the learning process, for teachers change as they observe students, reflect on their teaching and professional reading, and dialogue with a colleague. The following snapshots of the goal meetings with second-grade teacher Carol Chapman and science teacher Ray Legge illustrate the diverse needs of teachers and that a one-size-fits-all type of evaluation cannot stimulate growth and change among an entire staff.

Meeting with Carol Chapman

On a hot and lazy July afternoon, Carol and I meet at school; we lunch and chat in her air-conditioned room. A master teacher with more than twenty-five years' experience, Carol is a risk taker who was one of the first teachers at Powhatan to transform her primary classroom into a reading-writing workshop. She turns to students for evaluation of her strengths and needs as a teacher. "I value their input," she tells me. "They're always honest and make me reflect on what's happening as we work together." Over lunch, Carol hands me a piece of paper headed "Strengths and Weaknesses as a Teacher." On her own, Carol compiled this list because she believed it would support her evaluation.

"This list," she tells me, "contains strengths that I perceive, and a list of weaknesses that my second graders identified throughout the past year. These might affect the goals I establish."

Carol Chapman's Teaching Strengths

- a willingness to try new strategies and ideas
- a rapport with the children: the flexibility to meet the academic and emotional needs of every child
- the ability to create of a safe, positive atmosphere where children can and do succeed
- a good listener and observer

Needs Students Identified

- Teacher should negotiate periods of quiet time while they work and think. In Carol's class this is now called Maggie's Law, after the student who lobbied for quiet during writing workshop and math.
- Teacher should explain directions more thoroughly and record these on the chalkboard.
- Teacher should provide more time for free reading.
- Teacher should have regular class meetings and schedule extra meetings soon after children write notes that one is needed.
- Teacher should post a daily schedule.

We discuss the list, and Carol explains, "I have to carve out more free reading time and be responsive to students' call for class meetings, where they raise and discuss social concerns. Sometimes, it's difficult for me to interrupt workshop for a class meeting. These two items will be on my goal list." Next, Carol and I discuss a book I recommended she read: *On Their Way: Celebrating Second Graders as They Read and Write* by Jane Fraser and Donna Skolnick (1994). "I've already adopted one idea from the book," explains Carol, obviously excited about trying something new. "I mailed a postcard to every second grader, inviting them to bring in a favorite book they read this summer. During the first days of school, students will sit in the author's chair (Robb 1994), present a book talk, and collect future reading ideas from one another."

Carol brainstorms possible goals during the rest of our meeting. I ask her to reflect on her long list of twelve items, select five to six that she feels strongly about, and mail them to me in a week or two. Before I leave Carol says, "I've read *Guided Reading: Good First Teaching for All Children* by Irene Fountas and Gay Su Pinnell (1996). It's so rich that I'll have to reread parts many times in August and during the year if I'm going to start guided reading."

Nodding, I tell Carol, "I've reread sections of that book several times— let's discuss the first three chapters before school starts and continue discussing key sections all year."

Ten days later, Carol mails me this list of goals:

a. Have parent involvement in portfolio assessments, which by November become student-led parent-teacher conferences.

b. Hold regular class meetings and additional ones that respond to the children.

   c. Include more writing in math.

   d. Move small-group instruction to the guided-reading model that Fountas and Pinnell present.

   e. Try new ideas that Laura and I negotiate.

   f. Keep parental anxiety levels about children's progress low.

In addition to guided-reading groups, the new ideas that Carol implemented grew out of her reading *Mosaic of Thought: Teaching Comprehension in a Reader's Workshop* by Ellin Keene and Susan Zimmermann (1998). To her reading-strategy demonstrations, Carol added personal, book-to-book, book-to-community, and book-to-world connections, broadening students' thinking and creating meaningful purposes for reading.

Meeting with Ray Legge

It's mid-August. I open the door to the science lab and see Ray Legge stroking the head of a long black snake. I smile. More than twenty years ago, Ray was in my fifth-grade class, and I recall the spiders, snakes, crickets, and injured birds he brought to our room. Now, his classroom is like a mini-museum of the ecosystem surrounding Powhatan. Ray started his science career as a forest ranger in Virginia's national parks. For more than ten years, he's been teaching science at Powhatan in grades six and eight, as well as supporting teachers in the primary and middle grades.

After a tour of the lab and a close look at the beehive Ray has installed not too far from the lab's windows, we talk about the upcoming evaluation year. "One of my goals has come out of the new schedule," Ray explains. "Because the lab comfortably holds fourteen to fifteen students, classes have been split, and each section meets four times a week. This year, besides split sections, I'll have twenty-two sixth graders and twenty-five eighth graders once each week. I'd like to figure out projects that will take groups out of the lab."

"Have you considered involving your students with children in the primary grades?"

"I've never done cross-grade projects," says Ray. "It seems like a lot to manage with so many students."

We discuss helping third and fourth graders develop some independent hands-on experiences. After reading *Science Workshop: A Whole Language Approach* (Saul et al. 1993), Ray wanted to bring more hands-on learning to the middle grades. Finally, Ray decides to try three and sets cross-grade projects as his primary goal for the year:

1. Eighth graders will research inventors and create a deck of nonfiction cards for third grade.

2. Sixth graders will work with second graders, browsing through, exploring, and reading poems about the natural world.

3. Teams of eighth graders will create several science studies in a shoe box that third and fourth graders can explore.

A week later, Ray places three additional goals on my desk:

- Incorporate more technology.
- Try several vocabulary strategies.
- Implement two to three new hands-on experiences in grade six that relate to required curriculum in life sciences.

As the year progressed, Ray's students asked to participate in more cross-grade projects. A responsive listener, Ray adjusted his third goal: he prepared sixth graders to help kindergarten and first-grade students with hands-on life science studies. Maintaining a flexible stance enables teachers to shift gears, respond to what's working, create experiences that excite students, and still complete required curriculum.

Meeting with Ann Kiernan

"I thought you'd like to see what I invited Jenny [Ann's peer evaluator] to do," Ann Kiernan says as she hands me a checklist she prepared for Jenny Kronfeld, a highly skilled kindergarten teaching assistant. "I wanted Jenny to monitor these items during several observations, identify areas that need more consistency, and make sure that I don't call on the same people all the time." Improving classroom management was one of the goals Ann established with Jenny. To provide feedback for Ann, Jenny visited Ann's room six times between October and January, completing forms that listed Ann's seventh-grade reading-writing workshop students on the left and these headings across the top:

- Folders Passed Out
- Students Called on in Whole-Class Discussions
- Spokespersons for Small-Group Discussions
- Met with Individual Students
- Students Share Written Work Before Whole Group
- Computer Use

Many teachers include classroom management as a yearlong goal, for management style affects students' participation and learning. From these checklists, Ann recognized that her contact with individual students concentrated on struggling readers and writers, and she worked diligently to confer with all students each week.

Setting goals provides the foundation for a positive yearlong partnership. Through observations, study, conferences, and formal and informal discussions, growth and change occur.

Observe, Confer, Study, Discuss

When I agree to peer evaluate a colleague, I complete two to three impromptu visits, walk around the room, chat with and help students, and look at displays and folders. Impromptu visits are from ten to twenty minutes and occur during a free period or in the morning as students arrive and prepare for the day. My goal is for students to feel comfortable when I'm there and to accept me as another teacher. Though not required by the evaluation guidelines, several short visits offer me glimpses into classroom atmosphere, students' work, and teacher-student interactions. Before each formal observation, one that I will write up for the teacher and her division head, the teacher and I set a purpose that connects to the teacher's goals.

In September, Carol Chapman wove two goals into students' learning experiences: (1) teaching reading for strategies and helping nineteen second graders make book-to-book and personal connections, and (2) creating authentic reading-writing centers and teaching children to use each one.

I observed about forty minutes of Carol's reading workshop on two consecutive days and wrote up my notes using the Classroom Observation Form that follows.

Observation Summary for: Carol Chapman

Dates observed: 9/9, 9/10

Focus of the observation(s): Reading Workshop

Purposes: To observe Carol's minilessons for predicting and making personal connections to the book; to observe students working in pairs, predicting the content of their books.

Strengths observed:

- Carol's demonstrations are clear; she uses enticing books, such as *The Garden of Abdul Gasazi* by Chris Van Allsburg (1979); she involves the children in her demonstrations to help them make personal connections.

- She repeats predicting demonstrations, knowing children need to hear and observe a minilesson many times.
- She asks children to question and comment on her demonstration.
- After the minilesson, Carol prints guidelines for children on chart paper and reviews these. I notice that the children refer to the chart when they practice.
- Carol opened the second class by asking: Do you remember what we learned about predicting and making personal connections yesterday? Was it hard/easy? Why?
- Children have many books to choose from for practicing with a partner. Books are easy reading so they can focus on the strategy.
- Children are open about how much they love reading and sharing their problem-solving strategies.
- When children worked in pairs, they used questions to help partners find support for predictions and make personal connections after completing the book.
- When an issue arises in class, such as how to correctly write titles, Carol has a minilesson at that moment, immediately responding to students.
- While children have a snack, Carol discusses "next steps" with me, not because she doesn't know what to do, but because she believes that collaborative discussions and problem solving will benefit her students.

Some questions to think about:

When you ask children for their predictions about a book, can you try to make your question as nondirective as possible? Instead of asking, "Could the boy be scared?" perhaps you can say, "Look at the boy and tell me what you notice about him," or "What might the boy be thinking or feeling?" Asking children what they notice is open-ended and nudges them to think with minimal teacher cues.

Notes from follow-up conference:

Carol and I discussed all the positives I observed. She's happy with the way students work in pairs, especially because they are making personal connections to the story. "I can't wait to introduce book-to-book connections," she says.

We discuss posing questions that are open-ended, and Carol asks me to monitor her questioning whenever I'm in the room. I told Carol that her awareness of this issue will also support framing open-ended questions.

Carol told me that her upcoming minilessons will focus on two areas: providing a journal model for students to write their predictions and support and modeling reading with expression.

When I compose an observation, I always emphasize as many positives as possible and list these first. All teachers, including myself, thrive on validation. Like our students, we can only build on strengths. Because I want to offer teachers choices and stimulate reflection, I select one need and express it as a query. Questions are less threatening than statements and have a gentler tone. It's crucial to be sensitive to a peer's feelings, especially if you want to provoke change.

Reading and discussing professional materials balances the *observe* and *confer* elements of peer evaluation with theory and research. It's my responsibility as a peer evaluator to suggest articles and books for reading and discussing. However, the teacher being evaluated also suggests reading materials. The goal of reading and discussing is to enlarge background knowledge so that teachers can make informed decisions while working with students.

Improving Teaching and Students' Learning

As teachers try research-supported strategies and dialogue with a peer, they improve as professionals, which in turn can boost students' progress and deepen students' and teachers' understanding of their own literacy processes. The peer-evaluation stories that follow illustrate one of the positive changes each teacher accomplished while participating in a yearlong evaluation-as-growth program.

Student-Led Parent-Teacher Conferences

Originally, Carol Chapman hoped to have her first student-led parent conferences in December. At a planning meeting with me for preparing students to lead conferences, Carol confided, "I'm not ready. I need more time to think about the process and help my second graders prepare to take the lead."

"That's fine," I said. "The goal here is for you to introduce this idea when *you* feel ready; there's no pressure to complete this goal by December." Carol's strong belief that student-led conferences would deepen her students' knowledge of their progress in reading and writing nudged her to continue reflecting on how to train students.

In mid-January, Carol and her students began preparations for March conferences. Students collaborated to compose the following letter of invitation to parents, which Carol typed and mailed in February. "I want parents to have plenty of time to fit these into busy schedules," she said.

Dear Parents,

During conferences, which begin on March 2, your child will participate fully in the discussions of his or her progress in the second grade. Therefore, make the appointment with the fact in mind that you will be bringing your child to the conference. Your child will lead the discussion concerning guided reading goals, the writing folder, the math graph, the reading response journals, and samples from the portfolio.

Your response to the conference will be shared in a letter to me and one to your child commenting on the positive things that you noticed at the conference. Please write the letter in the library immediately after the conference and place it in the tray by the second grade classroom door.

If you have any questions or concerns about this plan, please do not hesitate to contact me. I am anxious and excited to try this kind of reporting. The children are aware of their strengths and goals in the classroom and hopefully will be able to inform you successfully. This will be a first for the second grade!

Sincerely,

Carol Chapman

Carol held three thirty-minute conferences a day and completed the cycle in six days. Students worked at literacy centers or read while she listened to each conference and took detailed notes. She also held some conferences after school. Here is Carol's summary of Lowell Brown conferring with his mother, Kate.

Conference Report
March 5
Lowell Brown

At this student-led conference, Lowell shared his growth and strengths in reading and writing with his mother and his teacher, Mrs. Chapman.

Lowell began with his guided reading goal, which is to use the text to confirm what he is sharing or answering. He gave an example from *My Father's Dragon* by Ruth Stiles Gannet. He then explained how we were studying Steven Kellogg using the KWL strategy and reading as many of his books as possible. He also explained his syllable juncture spelling group, and how they were working with homophones.

Lowell shared his writing workshop folder and read several stories and poems from it. He said that his illustrations are better, he is better about spacing his words, and his stories make more sense now than earlier in the year. He shared three pages from his reading response journal, saying that he has improved in spelling, that he explains ideas using more details, underlines titles of books, and capitalizes important words. He also enjoyed reading through his portfolio where he could see his growth in writing.

Lowell then shared his math graphs. On the initial addition graph, it shows that it took him four tries to do all thirty-six facts in less than two minutes. On the subtraction graph, it shows that he has gone from three and half to three minutes in three tries.

Lowell's mother wrote this note to Carol Chapman, offering a parent's perspective on student-led conferences.

March 5

Dear Carol,

I thought the conference format worked *very* well. I enjoyed seeing Lowell take pride in sharing his work with me. The outline and your organization was helpful. His father and I were pleased with his report and comments! He truly seems so much happier.

With sincere thanks,
Kate

After Carol completed all nineteen conferences, I interviewed her to collect her thoughts and feelings. What follows is a transcription of my notes.

Laura: How do you feel about student-led conferences now that you've completed the process?

Carol: It was worth all the work and anxiety. The children understood their progress and owned it as they talked to parents.

Laura: How did parents react?

Carol: Most were surprised that their child could discuss progress in reading, writing, and math. They loved having this feedback, asking the children questions, and receiving clear and detailed explanations.

Laura: Did any students have difficulty answering parents' impromptu questions?

Carol: Some did. But I was there to start them with a question that reminded them of an experience or detail, and then the children took over.

Laura: How did the children react?

Carol: At first, each child was nervous just thinking about leading a conference. Once they started talking, they said they forgot about being scared. When they finished, they felt great pride and more confident because I trusted them with a demanding task.

Laura: Can you tell me about the preparation process?

Carol: It took almost eight weeks to prepare everyone. I met [with each student] one-on-one and we discussed strengths and goals in reading and writing. This was easy because I confer with students all year, and we are setting goals and isolating strengths and comparing their work to the criteria we negotiate for writing workshop, journals, and responses to reading. It was a matter of choosing representative pieces from folders and journals, organizing them, and creating an agenda for them to talk from.

Laura: Did you have concerns as you prepared children?

Carol: Organizing reading-writing workshop time so students kept moving forward as I worked with individuals worried me. Preparation went smoothly because the children were comfortable completing literacy centers and reading silently. The children kept reading and writing folders all year and selecting pieces and goals was not difficult because we'd done it all year. The biggest challenge was myself. I've always done all the talking at conferences. This time I had to be a listener and say little to nothing. Taking notes on the conference changed my focus. Also, listening to the children was much more interesting than hearing my own voice.

Laura: Will you do this again?

Carol: Definitely. And I'm helping first-grade teacher Debi Gustin start student-led conferences.

The growth and confidence teachers gain through peer evaluation is infectious as they talk to colleagues and invite other teachers to observe. Often one teacher's enthusiasm for an achieved goal inspires another teacher to learn and try a new strategy. As more and more people gain experience with a strategy, the amount of expertise within a school grows and can stimulate additional change.

Cross-Grade Projects

After Ray Legge agreed to completing two, or possibly three, cross-grade projects between older and younger students, the first question he posed to me was, "Who organizes the project?"

"Do you have any thoughts?" I asked.

"It would help if students do the organizing."

Cereal

Have you ever heard the name "Kellogg" before?
Who - Will and Dr. John Kellogg
What - cereal
When –1894
Why – They were trying to come up with a health food for hospital patients.
Where – Battle Creek, Michigan

One day in 1894 Will and Dr. John Kellogg were boiling wheat kernels. When they were about to roll it into flat sheets they were interrupted and had to leave for a couple of days. When they returned they put the kernels through the rollers and it came out in separate flakes. Moisture had spread into the kernels and that had made the kernels come out in separate flake. Some related inventions are ground grains (flour) and bread. Books to Learn more – <u>Goodnight Moon</u> and <u>Three Little Bears</u>.

Figure 7–1. Katherine's inventor card. On the back side she cut and pasted the names of a variety of dry cereals from cereal boxes.

"I agree," I answered. "You might consider having them work in groups and plan guidelines for introducing the project to the lower grades."

"That will take more time," Ray said, thinking out loud.

"What will students learn from that kind of planning?"

"The process of completing the project, but also, how to effectively engage younger students," Ray said.

"It will take more time," I agreed. "I suggest you pilot doing it this way, keep detailed notes of class time and students' learning, and then decide whether or not you want to continue this way next year."

Ray agreed. When we met to discuss his observations, Ray noted that the planning taught sixth and eighth graders about finding and exploring poetry books in the library, using the *Reader's Guide to Periodicals,* designing the format of the cards about inventors, and logging on to the computer to discover titles in our library and explore the Internet for additional information (see Figure 7–1).

Planning presentations for younger children sent older students to the primary teachers to collect tips for teaching. Older students had to think through guidelines for completing the project, so they could effectively present these. Learning to respond to questions younger students posed meant that older students had to do impromptu thinking. All agreed that the more information they had and the more planning they'd completed, the easier it was to respond to unplanned queries.

Sixth and eighth graders evaluated cross-grade projects by responding to these items:

1. List what you learned by doing this project.
2. Did you feel that teaching the younger students was beneficial? Why?

3. Should upcoming sixth and eighth grades complete cross-grade projects?

The response to number three was a unanimous "YES." For the first item, students wrote long lists of new information learned. Most felt that continual work in the library raised their comfort levels with research and finding books. All gave high ratings to planning and teaching younger students. They agreed that to teach means you really have to know your topic. One student summed up the feeling of the majority, writing that planning and teaching made the project theirs (the students') instead of just another assignment from the teacher.

Writers' Notebooks

Before our first meeting in late August, I invited third-grade teacher Nancy Roche to read Joanne Hindley's *In the Company of Children* (1996). "Is there an idea in this book that you would like to try?" I asked.

Without hesitation, Nancy replied, "Writers' Notebooks" (Calkins with Harwayne 1991; Harwayne 1992, both discussed in Hindley 1996). Nancy agreed with my suggestion that she keep a notebook to experience the process and have entries to share with students. Nancy's introductory lesson included sharing an entry from her notebook and showing students a variety of possible notebooks they might consider purchasing.

In a Friday letter to parents, Nancy explained the purpose and benefits of young writers keeping notebooks and the importance of students choosing the kind they wanted. Monday morning, nineteen third graders marched into class brandishing notebooks and peppering Nancy repeatedly with "When do we begin writing?" Every day, sometimes several times a day, students write in their notebooks, collecting what Calkins and Harwayne call "seeds"—ideas for stories, poems, or articles they might write.

In the past, third graders who arrived early found a comfortable place in the classroom and read. Now, many choose writing in their notebooks during this time. "I'm much more of a reader than writer and more comfortable with teaching reading," Nancy told me. "I don't think I would have tried notebooks by myself. I like having someone to discuss students' reactions [with] and find ways to encourage the few who say, 'I don't have any ideas.'"

Nancy's comment sums up one of the powerful benefits of peers learning together: it's easier to take risks because support is always available through a conference at school, a quick chat during recess, or a telephone call in the evening. Educators agree that learning is social and interactive for children (Holdaway 1980; Cambourne 1988; Hynds 1997); it's the same for teachers and all adults.

Peer Evaluators Grow and Learn

A powerful by-product of peer evaluation is that the evaluator grows and learns by observing, conferring, and reading and discussing professional materials with a partner. While working with Ray Legge, I learned about motors, a topic I was totally ignorant of; simple machines; and owls. My peer-evaluation experiences altered my reading habits: now I regularly read science and math journals, professional materials I occasionally browsed through in the past.

In the following interview with Tim Brown, Powhatan's Spanish teacher, Tim explained what he learned after a goal-setting meeting, three formal observations, and follow-up conferences while peer evaluating Fabienne Modesitt, our French teacher.

Laura: How did you negotiate your first observation of Fabienne?

Tim: After we agreed upon a time, two days before my visit, Fabienne gave me a plan for that day as well as handouts.

Laura: How did that help you?

Tim: I read over the materials and had a feel for the lessons before observing. There was also enough time for me to ask Fabienne to clarify some points.

Laura: Has the peer evaluation helped your teaching?

Tim: Absolutely. Trained in France, Fabienne is a native speaker who sets high goals for students. During every class, her students listen to French tapes so they grow accustomed to hearing and comprehending a variety of French accents.

Laura: Can you do the same for Spanish students?

Tim: Yes. In fact, I've already ordered tapes for my classes.

Laura: Did you collect other strategies?

Tim: During each class, Fabienne always has students listen, read, write, and speak. Students always practice all four, and Fabienne plans her classes around these experiences. I am revisiting the experiences I offer students and trying to balance my preparations to include all four.

Tim pointed out that the process nudged him to question his teaching practices because he started to reflect on and evaluate the experiences he provided Spanish students. It also opened a beneficial dialogue between Fabienne and him, a practice he planned to continue beyond this year.

Some Drawbacks of Peer Evaluation

Occasionally peer evaluators feel the process has some drawbacks. A drawback that some teachers experience is the additional stress they feel when they have to make plans for a substitute before observing or meeting with a peer. For some, it's a challenge to start the evaluation process on time, then negotiate classroom visits over several months, instead of completing all the visits at the last minute. However, Powhatan's administrators agree that the benefits of peer evaluation are greater than any drawbacks. Moreover, if teachers communicate their frustrations, the administration should provide the necessary support to resolve any problems.

Administrators' View of the Process

Periodically, John Lathrop, Powhatan's Head, and I converse about the peer-evaluation process. Frustrated with a peer evaluator who by February had visited his partner's class only once, John and I discussed options. "My goal for the faculty is to have many opportunities to grow and improve at and away from school," John told me. "I expect that the process won't always work smoothly. I think it's important to ask why it's been difficult to negotiate class visits."

That afternoon, I met with the teacher. Again, I relearned an important lesson: asking a simple question such as "Can you tell me why you haven't been able to arrange classroom visits and conferences?" can ease my frustration and any negative assumptions that bombard my mind. The reply came quickly, "My husband's illness and my own class are all I can manage. I should have let the teacher know, but I kept hoping that the pressures would lessen." Posing a question is what I do with my students and it should be no different for adults. Explanations such as family or personal illness, a heavy workload from graduate classes, or a second job can create a feeling of "I can't do another thing." Since this experience, I've learned to communicate sooner with the teacher, trying to resolve the problem; waiting until February was too late to repair the process. There are times when extra support isn't enough, and I delay the evaluation a year. If there's time, I negotiate extending an invitation to another peer. At Powhatan, the heads of the lower and upper school are sympathetic to the need for balance in a teacher's life. Both agree that maintaining the flexibility to delay the process creates a nurturing and teacher-centered environment. Yearly interviews with Powhatan's upper and lower school heads open issues for the entire faculty to consider. The following is an excerpt from one such interview with the upper school head.

Laura: What advantages have you observed with peer evaluation?

Tom: It promotes professional development so much better than the old checklist. The process promotes self-reflection and learning with a peer you value. Both learn. It's one way to combat that feeling of isolation—working alone. Teachers give it high ratings because it's not adversarial.

Laura: How do you involve yourself with the process?

Tom: I dialogue with teachers after I receive write-ups of observations and follow-up conferences. I'm always available to cover classes so observations can occur.

Laura: How often do you cover classes?

Tom: Three to five times a month. The dollars [that otherwise would have been] spent on a substitute for one to two hours can be used for materials and books.

Laura: Do you have reservations about the process?

Tom: First, there is a variation in the effort of pairs, but I accept that because levels of commitment differ.

Laura: Any other concerns?

Tom: The model is for the classroom. What it doesn't assess and evaluate are recess and hall duties, arriving at school on time, school-home communication, and team efforts.

Laura: Aren't those areas that administrators can review?

Tom: Yes. In fact, I prefer addressing those issues in a conversation with the teacher that allows us to collaborate and resolve such issues.

During my interview with the head of lower school, she pointed out all the advantages that Tom had cited. She also presented a drawback that I brought to the faculty.

Laura: Do you see any disadvantages to this process?

Carolyn: Sometimes, there is a great variation in the commitment and follow-through made by a peer evaluator.

Laura: Can you give me examples?

Carolyn: Some teachers accept the invitation and then it's November and they haven't even had a goal meeting. When I have to remind and nag to get a teacher involved, it builds up resentment and frustration in me. Also, the teacher being evaluated does not receive the full benefit of the process.

Laura: Is that behavior the rule or exception in your division?

Carolyn: Usually, the exception. Although, this year, I have two peer evaluators who need constant prodding. It also makes the teacher being evaluated feel discomfort and frustration.

Carolyn's words replayed in my mind for many days. Rather than seek a solution with her, I decided to bring the issue to the faculty at a meeting. Teachers decided that at the end of each school year, we would invite faculty to sign up if they felt they could make a commitment to peer evaluation the next year. Teachers being evaluated would choose from that list. This solution gave potential peer evaluators choices annually and removed the pressure of having to be available all the time.

Peer evaluation focuses on classroom practices and empowers teachers to collaborate in order to learn about and risk trying new ideas. Administrators monitor the process and offer positive feedback through informal conversations and letters. When John Lathrop read the summary sheet of Carol Chapman's evaluation, he wrote this letter:

Dear Carol:

I have received from Laura the summary of your teacher evaluation. I was very pleased to receive it because of the excellent goals and the way you and Laura worked together towards achieving them. You have made real gains in guided reading. I often cite your work in math when I talk to prospective parents about our inquiry-based program. I love how you encourage and validate a diversity of ways to arrive at a correct answer. Parents felt that the student-led conferences in March were the best meetings about their child's work that they had experienced.

Laura is correct. You are a master teacher and children have a wonderful experience in your classroom. Over the next several years, you will have the opportunity to mentor several teachers new to Powhatan. They will gain a great deal from watching you teach and conferring with you.

Sincerely,

John

Closing Thoughts

If you plan to institute a peer-evaluation program in your school, you'll want to adapt the experiences at Powhatan to your school community. Though the idea for Powhatan's program came from a request issued by John Lathrop, the concept of peer evaluation as growth came from a faculty committee.

Once you have the school administration's approval for such a program, organize a group of teachers willing to design a program for your school. Know that the success of this program hinges on communication with and input from all teachers. Therefore, the entire faculty needs to adjust and evaluate the program annually. Evaluation should point to strengths and what worked first, then identify concerns. Honest and open communication is your school's insurance for building a program that meets the changing and evolving needs of every teacher and child.

8

Moving Forward with Professional Study

A friend and colleague who is a principal in another state called to vent about a required staff development day for elementary and middle school teachers planned by the new director of instruction. One hundred fifty teachers attended a morning and an afternoon session held in the middle school auditorium. Teachers and principals were not consulted about their needs or the topics each expert presented. Everyone departed both sessions frustrated and angry, for the morning speaker discussed prior knowledge and reading comprehension and the afternoon speaker talked about writing assessment, K to 8. Not only were the presentations too broad to affect all grades, but teachers in these schools had been learning in study groups and had absorbed a great deal of background knowledge on both topics. Had principals and teachers been consulted, professional study could have been arranged that would have enlarged their knowledge, rather than repeating what they had already learned through dedicated, collaborative study.

I relate this story because all over the country, valuable dollars are spent on the traditional inservice model, with a one-size-fits-all, one-time presentation that does not support teacher growth and student improvement. It's similar to the one-size-fits-all set of standards (Ohanian 1999) that Virginia and other states have imposed on teachers and students. The assumption is that intellectual development and ability and prior knowledge and experiences are the same for everyone. This assumption leads proponents of rigid standards to conclude that we learn the same way and at the same rate. Public school systems such as Virginia's, with high-stakes testing programs that plan to punish lower-achieving schools by withdrawing state accreditation and removing principals, pace students' learning and march on with covering curriculum, even if students struggle with the material.

In populations all over the world, the diversity of intellectual abilities and life experiences differs widely. Rather than focus on one set of standards and one literacy program that fits few, state legislators need to understand that effective teaching recognizes that students require different methods of teaching and learning at different points in their lives (Duffy and Hoffman 1999).

I'm not surprised that it's difficult to change administrators' and many teachers' view of effective teaching and professional study, for past experiences tend to influence the educational model we adopt. In the November 1999 issue of *Language Arts*, Nicholas J. Karolides makes this point in a conversation with Louise Rosenblatt, the renowned educator who developed reader-response theory. Recently, Rosenblatt received the 1999 National Council of Teachers of English Outstanding Educator in the Language Arts Award for all of her contributions to literacy. Rosenblatt told Karolides, "It's natural to teach the way we've been taught. I understand how much we are dominated by what we have assimilated from our environment—*that even after we accept new ideas, it's not easy to develop new patterns of behavior*" (161, italics are mine). It's the responsibility, then, of teacher-training institutions to recognize what Rosenblatt points out and to shape preservice teacher programs so that they provide undergraduate and graduate experiences based on the research of how children and adults learn best.

At large universities and colleges, future teachers sit through classes in lecture halls filled with two to three hundred students. They observe and listen to the professor deliver long speeches on television monitors and take multiple-choice tests graded by computers. Even in small colleges with small classes, the lecture method persists. All teacher-training programs must move from the delivery model to a collaborative, hands-on model, in which learners have the opportunity to reinvent knowledge (Wells 1986). Then administrators and teachers can use their prior knowledge and experiences to deepen their understanding of the need for professional study that promotes lasting and effective change among teachers and students.

Initiating and Developing Professional Study Programs

Administrators are not the only ones who can begin a professional study program. At Powhatan, teachers initiated a study of writing workshop and brought about significant change. The idea for change started at the grassroots level, but the administrators quickly supported teachers' efforts to learn. Though it is difficult to effect change without a principal's support, it is not impossible.

Study groups can be organized by teachers and materials can be obtained from area libraries or purchased by group members. In one school, kindergarten teachers studied emergent literacy at breakfast meetings in a local coffee shop. Once a month they scheduled a potluck dinner at a different teacher's home and collaborated over a meal. At these meetings they learned together but also supported one another when questions arose about bringing a strategy such as interactive writing to their classrooms.

Two months before school ended, these teachers invited the principal to attend their potluck dinner. Not only did the principal enjoy the evening, she also observed the benefits of these teachers' collaborations. The following year, the principal invited kindergarten teachers to help her initiate study groups for all grades. Here are some suggestions for initiating change in the type of professional study your school chooses:

- Meet on your own time.
- Support one another by offering positive feedback for risk taking.
- Visit one another's classrooms to provide feedback.
- Establish clear and productive study-group procedures before inviting the principal or another administrator to participate.
- Ask the principal to attend a meeting that will interest him or her.
- Invite the principal into your classroom so he or she can observe the benefits of collaborating with colleagues. Show samples of students' work and invite the principal to converse with students.

Professional study for teachers is as important as schooling and learning is for the children they teach. By including principals and their assistants in the learning process, it's possible over time to improve the way children learn, think, and problem solve.

Changing the Landscape: Interviews with Two Principals

Ann Conners, principal of Keister Elementary School, and I reviewed the school's progress after my fifth year of teaching and learning with her faculty. I also met with my son, Evan, principal of Warren County Junior High School, and asked him to review his first-year professional study goals. The excerpts that follow from both interviews emphasize the importance of ongoing study that reaches the diverse experience levels of all teachers. In the first excerpt, Ann Conners discusses the long-term effects that professional study has had on students, teachers, and administrators at her school.

Laura: From your perspective, how have the past five years affected teachers?

Ann: My teachers realized that reading and writing strategies continually evolve. Over the years, I've observed that as teachers thought more about their own literacy and systematically observed their students, their knowledge of certain strategies deepened. Teachers now adapt minilessons to their students' needs. Among some teachers, I saw a willingness to be introspective, to read professional books, and to reflect on their teaching practices and beliefs. Continuous study enabled teachers to develop a literacy theory and a greater awareness of how and why teachers make instructional decisions. Others took risks more readily and gained confidence in their teaching because you, Joe Nicholas, and I were always there to support them.

Laura: Have you observed long-term improvement of instruction?

Ann: There's consistently more modeling of reading strategies and writing techniques throughout a themed study or while reading a book. Large charts with strategy lessons students are studying hang on classroom walls. Students use these and teachers refer to them. All grades, K to 5, now use interactive word walls across the curriculum. These are accessible to students so children can attach words onto the wall and select words with common meanings, rhymes, endings, et cetera.

Laura: Can you give me one or two examples?

Ann: In the gymnasium, Barbara Cavanaugh, our physical education teacher, has word walls for different grades that cover major bones in the skeletal system, the elements of physical fitness, and different body shapes and positions. Physical education word walls change with the sport students are working on and often enrich a health study in the classroom. Classroom teachers shared their knowledge of words walls with the physical education teachers during study groups, and this collaboration resulted in celebrating literacy on the walls of our gymnasium.

Laura: Can you give me examples of changes in students' performance?

Ann: On the literacy predictor test the fourth grade takes, more students earned a perfect score in writing style, voice, and organization since ongoing professional study has become part of our daily life.

Laura: How has communication among teachers improved?

Ann: At Keister, I think that communication has always been good. Literacy topics are now part of our exchanges. Teachers discuss reading strategies, flexible grouping, writing techniques, and professional articles. They share minilessons and have adopted a consistent vocabulary to use while teaching reading and writing. There's more interest in and conversations about what other teachers are doing, and teachers observe one another.

Laura: How has this literacy initiative affected your relationship with teachers?

Ann: I feel that I have learned so much about how children learn to read and write. Teachers see me attend every study-group session with you, and I join support groups. I've completed the same assignments, learned to take and interpret running records, and led guided-reading groups. With this knowledge, I can support teachers in their classrooms and better converse with teachers about literacy practices. During conferences with teachers, I now ask better questions.

Laura: Do you feel teacher study groups have become a tradition?

Ann: There is always a conflict between teachers feeling the need to have more time to work in their classrooms and the need for ongoing study. I would like to figure out a way to have study groups meet during the school day—perhaps an early dismissal twice a month—though the city would have to approve that decision for all elementary schools because of busing students home. Then study groups could occur more frequently and teachers would learn more. The format—teachers sharing a strategy or students' work—is great, for we learn from one another.

Laura: What benefits have you observed from participating in and monitoring teacher study groups?

Ann: Actually, I've changed faculty meetings into modified study groups. Out of one hour, I've limited announcements to ten minutes. At each meeting two to three teachers volunteer to share a lesson and then others raise questions and discuss issues that arise. On my daily rounds of visiting classrooms, I'll invite a teacher to discuss something I saw that worked well. Sometimes, I extend an invitation to share during a post-observation conference. This structure has received high ratings from teachers. I feel that observing their colleagues has provided the nudge several needed to risk trying something new. The atmosphere during these meetings is safe, positive, and upbeat.

Laura: Do you have a plan for continuing the momentum of professional study at Keister?

Ann: We have a district science consultant working with teachers who invite him into their classrooms. During the sixth year of our literacy initiative, you will be coming five times to work with teachers who request additional support and to strengthen guided-reading programs and flexible grouping.

Laura: Any other comments?

Ann: These five years have created significant changes in my own professional growth. Faculty meetings at Keister used to be dominated by me. I lectured and presented administrative information. Now, teachers do the talking, and I listen, question, and learn. I've come to value teachers even more and understand the challenges their job presents. I see the importance of taking risks and learning from mistakes. I am not the expert; I learn from children, from teachers, and by reading. If I want teachers to invest in professional study, then I need to listen to their suggestions and join their study groups. To be an effective instructional leader, a principal must be in close touch with teachers and students and become immersed in ongoing learning. That's the most satisfying part of leading a school.

I've included the following conversation with Evan Robb so you can see how far a new school can travel during the first year when the administration takes the lead in addressing, valuing, and encouraging professional study. The questions I posed grew out of phase 1 of the four-phase plan Evan and his staff had developed before school opened (see pages 31–33).

Laura: What professional study goals have you already met?

Evan: The summer before our new school opened, department chairs and experienced teachers met to create a peer-partner program. This was particularly important to Warren County Junior High because it was a new school with many teachers new to Warren County. That program is in place.

Laura: What about your peer-coaching goals?

Evan: Those took longer to put into practice. There are some coaching opportunities in the peer-mentoring plan, but some teachers definitely needed more support. Each month the assistant principal, dean of students, and I met with the department chair heads to discuss curriculum, materials they needed, and how to coach teachers. Since it was difficult for department heads, who have a full teaching load, to visit classrooms during the first three months of school, I spent most of every day in different classrooms, working alongside teachers and supporting students. I see my role as the instructional leader of this school and continue to enlarge my knowledge of effective teaching practices so I can assist teachers. I am rarely in my office.

Laura: What did you do to support teachers who would benefit from coaching?

Evan: New teachers have no choice, for a willingness to be coached was part of our agreement when I hired them. Department chairs identified experienced teachers who could and wanted to coach. Someone from the administrative team covered a coach's class, freeing the teacher to support a colleague. I have a strong teaching background in reading-writing workshop and believe that every administrator needs to stay in touch with students' learning styles, managing a classroom, and the behavior issues middle school teachers deal with daily. We're not reaching everyone during this first year, but we have begun a program that we will evaluate, expand, and improve annually.

Laura: Are departments meeting regularly to learn together?

Evan: Absolutely. Department heads negotiated the best times to meet with their staff. Every department meets for professional study at least once a month. Some, like the English department, meet twice each month. Teachers share what they are doing. They're encouraged to try new strategies and read professional articles. I will come into a classroom to support any teacher who asks for help. As soon as our library is in order, there will be a professional section for teachers. Departments have already given the librarian titles of books and magazines they'd like.

Laura: Do teachers grumble about early and after-school meetings?

Evan: At first, but not anymore.

Laura: Why do you think attitudes changed?

Evan: Teachers know that I work long hours to make this school a great place to learn for them and students. The assistant principal, dean of students, and I attend all department meetings and participate in professional study with teachers. We're in classrooms every day. The message that the three administrators work hard to improve students' learning and view teachers as professionals is out there. We've set aside budget money to send two to three teachers to state conferences in the spring. Next year, my goal is to send several teachers to state and national conferences. Ultimately, it's the students who benefit from professional study, and that's who we're here for.

Laura: Do departments that teach different subjects interact and support one another?

Evan: I'm glad you asked that question. In October, the English department invited me to a meeting. They believed it would help students if all teachers used the same heading on papers and standard editorial marks when correcting papers. They also wanted to encourage science and history teachers to have students write critical paragraphs and essays, so students would be writing across the curriculum. I encouraged the English teachers to plan a hands-on workshop for the faculty covering these ideas. To plan, they met several times before classes started. In December, the English department ran a terrific meeting, and the staff created a common heading for papers and agreed to use the same editing symbols. They also involved teachers in brainstorming, creating a writing plan, and demonstrated, by showing students' pieces, how detailed notes could improve students' writing. The staff received their presentation and suggestions enthusiastically. When teachers collaborate and teach each other, it's more meaningful than the principal stepping in and saying, "Do it this way." Part of my job is to know what to hand over to the faculty. The English department left the meeting knowing their colleagues appreciated their ideas. They also agreed to meet with content-area teachers, if this was necessary, to review writing strategies. All of this occurred because English teachers felt empowered to affect change.

Laura: Do you think the second part of your professional study plan that invites teachers to read professional articles, risk trying new strategies, and increases the number of teachers attending state and national conferences will fall into place as well as the first part?

Evan: As long as the administrators' goal is to make this happen, and we provide teachers with the training and materials they need, I am optimistic. The district has given me a budget for professional study for next year. Department heads will brainstorm suggestions that they will bring to the faculty. If I want teachers to invest in ongoing study, then they must be part of [the] decision-making process. Just as important is that dollars be spent on what teachers and students need most.

Effective teachers develop from collaborating, studying together, exchanging ideas, and teaching their students and one another. However, behind a productive professional study program you'll find a principal who understands that training and supporting teachers, not issuing proclamations, is the most effective way to improve students' learning.

In his prologue to *The Canterbury Tales,* Geoffrey Chaucer introduces the Clerk from medieval Oxford. The young clerk, uninterested in worldly possessions and high positions, prefers to read and pray for the souls of those who gave him the ability to study and learn. Chaucer ends his introduction of the Clerk with these words: "And gladly wolde he lerne and gladly teche," words that link studying to teaching, words that celebrate the spirit of ongoing professional study for teachers and administrators.

Closing Thoughts

For a professional study program to reach the needs of every teacher in a school, the principal must support the concept and fully participate in the learning experiences. An enlightened principal is a leader and collaborator and does the following:

- listens to teachers
- responds to teachers' desire to organize ongoing professional study
- includes teachers in the decision-making process for professional study
- understands that improved instruction benefits children's learning
- recognizes that assimilating new ideas is a slow process and takes time

- provides time for change and constructs a safe environment for teachers and students
- works side by side with teachers to encourage risk taking
- comprehends the benefits of peer mentors and coaches
- finds budget dollars to educate, not dictate policies

Finally, an effective principal is like the leader Lao-tzu, a Chinese philosopher who lived more than twenty-five hundred years ago, described below in this excerpt from *The Way of Life According to Lao-tzu* (Bynner, Witter 1976, #17 unpaged).

> A leader is best
> When people barely know he exists,
> Not so good when people obey and acclaim him.
> But of a good leader, who talks little
> When his work is done, his aim fulfilled,
> They will say "We did this ourselves."

Appendix A
Conference Form for Students

Form for Reading and Writing Conferences with Students

Form for Reading and Writing Conferences with Students

Name _____ Date _____

_____ Reading Conference   _____ Writing Conference

Topic to be discussed:

Positive points discussed by the teacher:

Points the teacher and student discussed:

List how the student plans to use information:

Do you need to schedule a follow-up conference?

Date of this conference:

Additional notes:

Appendix B
Surveys for Teachers

Professional Study Survey for Teachers
Reading-Writing Workshop Survey, K–2
Reading-Writing Workshop Survey, 3–5
Needs-Assessment Survey for Teachers
Teacher Evaluation of Professional Study Programs

Professional Study Survey for Teachers

List the words and phrases that come to mind after reading the plan for professional study:

List teaching strategies and/or projects that you would like to share with colleagues in your department:

List the professional magazines you would like our library to have:

List professional books you feel belong in the professional library for teachers:

List books for students that you would like to see in our school library:

Name _____ Date _____

Reading-Writing Workshop Survey, K–2

Directions: After reading this list of topics that could be covered at the two-day workshop, please select the top five items and number these, with 1 being the most important to you and 5 the least important.

Feel free to add topics that you feel should be addressed.

_____ Running records: symbols, use of

_____ Dynamic grouping of students for reading instruction based on teacher observation and running records

_____ The morning message and other shared writing experiences

_____ Shared reading: genres, "What do you notice?" strategy

_____ Writing workshop: getting started

_____ Word walls: interactive, punctuation, vocabulary, word families

_____ Reader's chair

Additional suggestions:

Reading-Writing Workshop Survey, 3–5

Directions: After reading this list of topics that could be covered at the two-day workshop, please select the top five items and number these, with 1 being the most important to you and 5 the least important.

Feel free to add topics that you feel should be addressed.

_____ Organizing a reading workshop

_____ The role and presentation of minilessons

_____ Key reading strategies: personal connections, visualization, predict/support/confirm/adjust, rereading, using context clues to figure out unfamiliar words, making inferences

_____ Writing workshop: getting started, organization, management

_____ Planning writing

_____ Narrative and expository writing

_____ Literature discussion groups

_____ Choosing books for instruction: novel study, core book plus extensions, groups read at students' independent level

_____ Having each student read a different book at his or her independent level and connecting books by a common theme, author, or topic

_____ Vocabulary instruction before, during, and while reading

_____ Open-ended, easy-to-implement journal responses

_____ Evaluating reading

_____ Evaluating writing

Additional suggestions:

Needs-Assessment Survey for Teachers

In the space at the left of the question, rate each question by writing one of the letters from the key.

Key: N = Never   R = Rarely   S = Sometimes   M = Most of the Time   A = Always

_____ Do students collaborate to problem solve and learn?

_____ Are there cross-grade projects?

_____ Do teachers use reading workshop?

_____ Do teachers use writing workshop?

_____ Does your school have peer partnerships?

_____ Does your school have coaches?

_____ Do teachers attend state and national conferences?

_____ Do teachers build consensus among themselves?

_____ Are teachers studying together?

_____ Is time set aside in the school's schedule for teacher study groups?

_____ Do teachers collaborate to plan themes and lessons?

_____ Do teachers share resources?

_____ Do teachers respect diverse learning styles?

_____ Is there pressure to cover curriculum even if children don't understand what they are learning?

_____ Is the principal visible each day?

_____ Does the principal attend and participate in professional study programs?

_____ Is the principal available to meet with teachers?

_____ Does the principal regularly visit and work in classrooms?

_____ Are curricular decisions collaborative?

_____ Does the principal build consensus for decisions that affect teachers?

Additional comments:

Teacher Evaluation of Professional Study Programs

I. List below the areas you like and areas that concern you.

Likes   *Concerns*

II. For each positive item on your list, explain why you would like to see that program continue. For each concern, brainstorm a list of possible solutions.

III. List other professional study components that you feel would assist you in teaching more effectively.

Appendix C
Forms for the Literacy Links Program

Checklist I of Storybook Reading Behaviors
Log of Storybooks Read Each Week
Checklist II of Storybook Reading Behaviors
Teacher's Observational Note Form

Checklist I of Storybook Reading Behaviors

Name _____ Grade _____

Behaviors   *Date Observed*

_____ Listens well.

_____ Asks questions.

_____ Discusses pictures.

_____ Points to items in pictures.

_____ Asks to hear story again.

_____ Knows front and back covers.

_____ Knows title.

_____ Knows title page.

_____ Knows dedication.

_____ Makes sensible predictions.

Additional comments:

Log of Storybooks Read Each Week

Week of _____

Title and Author   *Number of Times Read*

Monday:

_____

_____

_____

Tuesday:

_____

_____

_____

Wednesday:

_____

_____

_____

Thursday:

_____

_____

_____

Friday:

_____

_____

_____

Checklist II of Storybook Reading Behaviors

Name _____ Grade _____

Behaviors   *Date Observed*

_____ Points to a word.

_____ Points to spaces between words.

_____ Points to uppercase letters.

_____ Points to lowercase letters.

_____ Points to a period.

_____ Points to a question mark.

_____ Knows to read print from left to right.

_____ Knows that the words tell the story.

_____ Pretend reads.

Additional comments:

Teacher's Observational Note Form

Child's Name _____

Date of Observation _____

Describe the child's drawing:

Did the child scribble write?

Note the letters the child wrote:

Were there spaces between the letters?

List any words the child wrote:

Did the story the child told about his or her drawing match the pictures?

Write what the child said:

Did the story have a beginning, middle, and end?

Additional comments:

Appendix D
Forms to Use with Study Groups

Suggested Study-Group Topics
Goal and Debriefing Record
Summary Sheet for Study Groups

Suggested Study-Group Topics

This is a list, generated by teachers, for possible study-group topics.

Directions: Select seven items and rate them this way: 7 is what you'd like to participate in the most and 1 the least.

_____ Middle school literature

_____ Effective integration of technology in the classroom

_____ Web sites

_____ Word study and word sorts

_____ Guided reading in grades 3–5

_____ Planning interdisciplinary topics

_____ Class management: groups, one-on-one

_____ Interactive writing

_____ Computer training

_____ Teachers-as-readers group

_____ Assessment and evaluation

_____ Word walls

_____ Class meetings

_____ Writing: bringing each child along

_____ Signs among students of drug/alcohol abuse

_____ Maximum use of library facilities

_____ Integrating study strategies in the curriculum

_____ Portfolio assessment

_____ Spelling

_____ Developing effective history simulations

_____ Different methods of research

_____ Multicultural projects

Directions: Rate these teacher-facilitated topics in order of importance, with 6 being the most important and 1 the least important:

_____ Library integration: book talks, new books

_____ Guided reading

_____ Web quest

_____ Reading strategies for content-area subjects

_____ Body image and eating disorders

_____ Problem solving in math

Goal and Debriefing Record

- Before starting, establish goals for each one-hour session.
- If it's necessary to read materials between staff development meetings, work with the group to achieve consensus.
- To integrate new ideas into your teaching practices, it is crucial to try these in your classes. Teachers can select one thing to try in their classes and quickly share at the next meeting. It is also helpful if teachers photocopy samples of some students' work and bring these to the group.
- Reserve five minutes at the end of each session to debrief. First ask teachers to discuss what worked, then offer some suggestions for improvement.

Goals: Date:

Presentations:

Assignment:

Debriefing:

What Worked   *Needs*

Summary Sheet for Study Groups

Date:

List members attending:

List books and/or articles you are using as resources:

Summarize in a list or paragraph what you covered:

Goal(s) for next meeting:

Assignment:

Appendix E
Peer-Evaluation Forms

First Meeting: Establishing Goals
Classroom Observation Form
End-of-Year Peer-Evaluation Summary Sheet
     for Administrators

First Meeting: Establishing Goals

Teacher's Name _____

Peer Evaluator's Name _____

Year of Evaluation _____

Date of the First Meeting _____

List the goals you established:

List the ways you plan to help the teacher meet these goals:

Additional comments:

Classroom Observation Form

Observation summary for:

Dates observed:

Focus of the observation(s):

Purposes:

Strengths observed:

Some questions to think about:

Notes from follow-up conference:

End-of-Year Peer-Evaluation Summary Sheet for Administrators

Teacher's Name _____

Peer Evaluator's Name _____

Year of Evaluation _____

List established goals:

Number of classroom visits and observations:

Number of meetings:

Summary of the high points of the observations:

Needs that were discussed and addressed:

Additional comments:

References

Bear, Donald R., Marcia Invernizzi, Francine Johnston, and Shane Templeton. 1996. *Words Their Way: Word Study for Phonics, Vocabulary, and Spelling Instruction.* Upper Saddle River, NJ: Merrill.

Birchak, Barb, Clay Conner, Kathleen Marie Crawford, Leslie H. Kahn, Sandy Kaser, Susan Turner, and Kathy Short. 1998. *Teacher Study Groups: Building Community Through Dialogue and Reflection.* Urbana, IL: National Council of Teachers of English.

Boomer, Garth. 1992. "Negotiating the Curriculum." In *Negotiating the Curriculum: Education for the 21st Century,* edited by Garth Boomer, Nancy Lester, Cynthia Onore, and Jon Cook. Bristol, PA: Falmer Press.

Bynner, Witter, ed. 1976. *The Way of Life According to Lao-tzu.* New York: Berkley Publishing Group.

Calkins, Lucy McCormick. 1986. *The Art of Teaching Writing.* Portsmouth, NH: Heinemann.

Calkins, Lucy McCormick, with Shelley Harwayne. 1991. *Living Between the Lines.* Portsmouth, NH: Heinemann.

Cambourne, Brian. 1988. *The Whole Story: Natural Learning and the Acquisition of Literacy in the Classroom.* Auckland, Australia: Ashton Scholastic.

Churchill, Flavia. 1996. "Collaborative Inquiry: The Practice of Professional Development." In *Research in the Classroom: Talk, Texts, and Inquiry,* edited by Zoe Donahue, Mary Ann Van Tassell, and Leslie Patterson, pp. 108–116. Newark, DE: The International Reading Association.

Cook, Jon. 1992. "Negotiating the Curriculum: Programming for Learning." In *Negotiating the Curriculum: Education for the 21st Century,* edited by Garth Boomer, Nancy Lester, Cynthia Onore, and Jon Cook. Bristol, PA: Falmer Press.

Crafton, Linda K. 1991. *Whole Language: Getting Started . . . Moving Forward.* Katonah, NY: Richard C. Owen.

Cullinan, Bernice E. 1992. *Read to Me: Raising Kids Who Love to Read.* New York: Scholastic.

Cunningham, Patricia M. 1995. *Phonics They Use: Words for Reading and Writing,* 2d ed. New York: HarperCollins College.

de Gasztold, Carmen Bernos. 1973. *Prayers from The Ark and The Creatures' Choir.* Translated from the French by Rumer Godden. Illustrations by Jean Primrose. New York: Penguin Books.

Delgado, Mary. 1999. "Lifesaving 101: How a Veteran Teacher Can Help a Beginner." *Educational Leadership* 56 (8): 27–29.

Duffy, Gerald G., and James V. Hoffman. 1999. "In Pursuit of an Illusion: The Flawed Search for a Perfect Method." *The Reading Teacher* 53 (1): 10–16.

Evans, Paula M., and Nancy Mohr. 1999. "Professional Development for Principals' Seven Core Beliefs." *Phi Delta Kappan* 80 (7): 530–32.

Fielding, Linda, and Cathy Roller. 1998. "Theory Becomes Practice at the Point of Interaction." *Primary Voices K–6* 7 (1): 2–8.

Fletcher, Ralph. 1993. *What a Writer Needs.* Portsmouth, NH: Heinemann.

Fountas, Irene, and Gay Su Pinnell. 1996. *Guided Reading: Good First Teaching for All Children.* Portsmouth, NH: Heinemann.

———. 1998. *Word Matters: Teaching Phonics and Spelling in the Reading/Writing Classroom.* Portsmouth, NH: Heinemann.

Fraser, Jane, and Donna Skolnick. 1994. *On Their Way: Celebrating Second Graders as They Read and Write.* Portsmouth, NH: Heinemann.

Frost, Robert. 1975. *The Poetry of Robert Frost.* New York: Henry Holt.

Gallo, Donald R., ed. 1990. *Center Stage: One-Act Plays for Teenage Readers and Actors.* New York: HarperCollins.

Goodlad, John L. 1994. *Educational Renewal: Better Teachers, Better Schools.* San Francisco: Jossey-Bass.

Graves, Donald. 1983. *Writing: Children and Teachers at Work.* Portsmouth, NH: Heinemann.

———. 1990. *Discover Your Own Literacy.* Portsmouth, NH: Heinemann.

———. 1994. *A Fresh Look at Writing.* Portsmouth, NH: Heinemann.

Grimm, Jacob. 1986. *Rumpelstiltskin.* Illustrated and retold by Paul O. Zelinsky. New York: Dutton.

Harwayne, Shelley. 1992. *Lasting Impressions: Weaving Literature into the Writing Workshop.* Portsmouth, NH: Heinemann.

Hindley, Joanne. 1996. *In the Company of Children.* York, ME: Stenhouse.

Holdaway, Don. 1980. *The Foundations of Literacy.* Portsmouth, NH: Heinemann.

Hole, Simon, and Grace Hall McEntee. 1999. "Reflection Is at the Heart of Practice." *Educational Leadership* 56 (8): 34–37.

Hynds, Susan. 1997. *On the Brink: Negotiating Literature and Life with Adolescents.* Newark, DE: The International Reading Association.

Joyce, Bruce R., and Beverly Showers. 1983. *Power in Staff Development Through Research on Training.* Arlington, VA: ASCD.

Karolides, Nicholas J. 1999. "Theory and Practice: An Interview with Louise M. Rosenblatt." *Language Arts* 77 (2): 158–70.

Keene, Ellin, and Susan Zimmermann. 1998. *Mosaic of Thought: Teaching Comprehension in a Reader's Workshop.* Portsmouth, NH: Heinemann.

Le Guin, Ursula K. 1988. *Catwings.* Illustrated by S. D. Schindler. Boston: Orchard.

Lindbergh, Anne Morrow. 1983. *Gift from the Sea.* New York: Vintage.

Murray, Donald M. 1982. *Learning by Teaching.* Portsmouth, NH: Boynton / Cook.

———. 1984. *Write to Learn.* New York: Holt, Rinehart & Winston.

Ohanian, Susan. 1999. *One Size Fits Few.* Portsmouth, NH: Heinemann.

Parry, Jo-Ann, and David Hornsby. 1988. *Write On: A Conference Approach to Writing.* Portsmouth, NH: Heinemann.

Powers, Brenda Miller. 1996. *Taking Note: Improve Your Observational Notetaking.* York, ME: Stenhouse.

Robb, Laura. 1994. *Whole Language, Whole Learners: Creating a Literature-Centered Classroom.* New York: William Morrow.

———. 1998. *Easy-to-Manage Reading & Writing Conferences.* New York: Scholastic.

———. 1999. *Easy Mini-Lessons for Building Vocabulary: Practical Strategies that Boost Word Knowledge and Reading Comprehension.* New York: Scholastic.

Samuels, Jay S., and Alan E. Farstrup. 1992. *What Research Has To Say About Reading Instruction,* 2d ed. Newark, DE: The International Reading Association.

Santa, Carol Minnick. 1997. "School Change and Literacy Engagement: Preparing Teaching and Learning Environments." From *Reading Engagement: Motivating Readers Through Integrated Instruction,* pp. 218–33. Newark, DE: The International Reading Association.

Saul, Wendy, Jeanne Reardon, Anne Schmidt, Charles Pearce, Dana Blackwood, and Mary Dickinson Bird. 1993. *Science Workshop: A Whole Language Approach.* Portsmouth, NH: Heinemann.

Stone, Sandra J. 1999. "A Conversation with John Goodlad." *Childhood Education: Infancy Through Early Adolescence* 75 (5): 264–68.

Taylor, Denny, and Dorothy S. Strickland. 1986. *Family Storybook Reading.* Portsmouth, NH: Heinemann.

Tell, Carol. 1999. "Renewing the Professions of Teaching: A Conversation with John Goodlad." *Educational Leadership* 56 (8): 14–19.

Van Allsburg, Chris. 1979. *The Garden of Abdul Gasazi.* Boston: Houghton Mifflin.

Vaughan, Joseph L., and Thomas H. Estes. 1986. *Reading and Reasoning Beyond the Primary Grades.* Boston: Allyn & Bacon.

Vygotsky, Lev S. 1978. *Mind in Society: The Development of Higher Psychological Processes.* Cambridge, MA: Harvard University Press.

Wasserman, Selma. 1999. "Shazam! You're a Teacher: Facing the Illusory Quest for Certainty in Classroom Practice." *Phi Delta Kappan* (February): 464–68.

Watson, Dorothy, ed. 1987. "Valuing and Evaluating the Learners and Their Language." In *Ideas and Insights: Language Arts in the Elementary School,* pp. 209–19. Urbana, IL: Nations Council of Teachers of English.

Wells, Gordon. 1986. *The Meaning Makers.* Portsmouth, NH: Heinemann.

Index